SOCIALIZATION

SOCIALIZATION
Process, Product, and Change

edited by

EDWARD Z. DAGER
University of Maryland

MARKHAM PUBLISHING COMPANY/Chicago

MARKHAM
READINGS IN SOCIAL PSYCHOLOGY SERIES
Michael A. Malec, editor

Dager, ed., *Socialization: Process, Product, and Change*
Malec, ed., *Attitude Change*
Malec, ed., *Collective Behavior*
O'Brien, ed., *Methods in Social Psychology: Current Perspectives in Behavioral Research*
Taylor, ed., *Small Groups*

To Janet, Michael, and Beth

Newman University
Library
Tel: 0121 476 1181 ext 1208

Borrowed Items 06/12/2018 17:37
XXXX0621

Item Title	Due Date
* Class, status, and power : social stratification in comparative perspective	02/01/2019 23:59
* Understanding Bourdieu	02/01/2019 23:59
* Socialization; process, product, and change	02/01/2019 23:59
Sociology in focus	17/12/2018 23:59

* Indicates items borrowed today
Thankyou for using Newman Library

www.newman.ac.uk/library
library@newman.ac.uk

Markham Readings in Social Psychology

There is a problem inherent in any collection of readings on a broad topic like social psychology: namely, that an editor, teacher, and student will never agree on what topics should be included, and with what emphasis. Our response to this is the Markham Readings in Social Psychology Series, which is not "just another reader," but a series of readers, each relatively small, but focused on a specific topic. The goal of this series is not to present a particular theoretical or methodological perspective in social psychology, but to provide the student with a substantial sampling of the important studies in a given area.

By covering the field of social psychology in a series of small volumes, several advantages are offered: (1) *flexibility*, since particular volumes may be selected for particular courses; (2) *expertise*, since each volume is compiled by an area specialist; and (3) *complementarity*, since the several volumes can be used together to provide a fairly complete coverage of social psychology.

The articles in this volume on SOCIALIZATION have been brought together to enable the reader to chart the entire path of the socialization process—from the necessary conditions for early identification (inculcation of personality traits, attitudes, and values)—through structural effects that facilitate or impede the socialization process. In the last section, social factors that create conditions conducive to change in the personality are examined.

Acknowledgments

I would like to express my appreciation to Robert A. Ellis and Larry L. Hunt for their critical comments on the manuscript, and to Laura A. Bonagura for her assistance in the time consuming task of bringing these materials together. I also thank the authors and publishers who have granted permission to publish their works.

Introduction

Socialization is the most efficient and effective means of social control. It is through the socialization process that the necessary ingredients for social order are instilled in the personality. Laws against such acts as homicide, drug use, assault, robbery, and embezzlement do not prevent their occurrence on a broad scale. Prevention, instead, is a function of individual traits that are "built into" the personality at an early age when children are taught that certain kinds of activities are right or wrong. When one generation fails to adequately fulfill its socialization mission, deviant acts begin to exceed the frequency tolerable to society. In this sense, social control is a by-product of socialization. This does not deny the fact that laws help to reinforce values and attitudes and make them more compelling. Nevertheless, the most effective means of limiting deviant acts disorganizing to society is to inculcate the young with values and attitudes that serve to perpetuate those elements in the social system deemed important by its members. When this process breaks down or is haphazard, faulty socialization occurs. The result is increased conflict between generations and departure from existing norms and accepted patterns of behavior.

It is important to note that no generation duplicates exactly the generation preceding. Imperfections and uncertainties in the socialization process make this impossible. (For an excellent discussion of the sources of change, see Moore, 1960.) Furthermore, most social systems, especially those based on democratic principles, need to provide latitude of expression to permit adaptation and creative changes necessary for the systems survival.

Socialization, broadly defined, is the process by which the infant learns the ways of a given social group and is molded into an effective participant (Dager, 1964). Because of imperfections in this process, the infant is not completely "molded," but in the course of his development he acquires behavior, attitudes, values, and other personality traits that are at once unique to him and at the same time characteristic of the group or groups that serve as the socializing agent.

Typically, the most important elements in socialization occur within primary groups and with individuals in face-to-face interaction, and are facilitated by the process called identification. Identification is the process by which the infant becomes or behaves like some other or others and/or like others expect. It involves psychological processes and includes motives, both conscious and unconscious. Without identification, the values and attitudes of adults will not be transmitted to the infant and the by-products of the identifactory process—imitation, role modeling, and so on—will be considerably diluted or distorted. Whether or not one identifies with another is a function of four fundamental conditions:

1. Interaction must occur between the infant and some adult or adults.
2. The adult(s) must be predisposed to satisfy the needs of the infant (nurturance).
3. A dependent relationship must develop between the infant and some adult or adults.
4. The adults must have control of the resources the infant needs or feels it needs (power to reward and punish).

Each of these four conditions are interrelated and must be operative in a given social relationship if identification is to occur. Thus, in an ideal adult-infant relationship, the adult is predisposed to satisfy the basic needs of an infant, and engages in activity designed to achieve this. This activity and interaction must be sufficiently consistent over a long period of time for dependency to develop. In addition to developing dependency, consistent behavior over a long period tends to stabilize the relationship and preclude development of extreme anxiety. During and following the above process, the adult, normally in control of the resources, dispenses them according to the desirability of the behavior performed by the infant. The infant will identify with the adult because he is dependent on him; in order to receive certain rewards and avoid punishment of various kinds the infant will be motivated to conform to expected behavior. This includes the learning of a language, the internalization of standards of acceptable and unacceptable behavior, values, attitudes, and so on. Moreover, since the interaction is consistent and continuous, the behavior and activity of the adult are openly visible to the child, facilitating imitation behavior and role modeling. These four conditions can be and often are conditioned, or in one way or another affected, by structural variables such as social class, size of family, occupation, and so on. Since the conditions and processes described are seldom perfectly executed, identification will vary by degree and intensity. In some cases of strong positive relationships, over-identification leads to over-dependence which tends to incapacitate the individual. In most instances, however, especially in highly complex societies, it is a low degree of identification that creates most of the problems.

Since socialization is a very broad field and encompasses contributions from a great variety of disciplines, no reader can do justice to the entire field. Consequently, the readings in this book deal with selective aspects of the social and emotional development of the child and some of the more strategic processes that facilitate the transmission of values and attitudes during the early years. Moreover, rather than focus upon individual researches, the articles were selected to provide a theoretical view of socialization, to depict significant variables in the study of socialization, or, although they are reports of specific research, to reflect some basic process by which values and attitudes are transmitted and or changed.

The lead article (Part I) by S. F. Nadel sets the tone and provides the perspective for the remainder of the readings by elucidating the processes by which one generation socializes the next. Nadel's eloquent argument explains how, through the guidance of societal values, rewards, and punishments, social control evolves into self-regulation, because "even societies relying on machineries of control . . . must rely also on values simply held," and public assertions of right and wrong must also be the private convictions of individuals in a viable social order. In this way Nadel points out the circularity of effect that exists between the culture and institutions, and the individual.

Part II is divided into two sections. In the first section, Eleanor Maccoby gives an intensive and insightful discussion of several classes of variables which have been in the forefront of the study of socialization. She points out those areas in which unexpected experimental results have exposed the variety of meanings certain socialization variables can have. In other words, findings from research studies are utilized to demonstrate that socialization variables can have several dimensions. Her discussion is designed to clarify divergent points of view.

In the same section, Lynn and Ellis provide a brief summary of their previous work, and each reinforces his own findings with data from other relevant research and presents some theoretical formulations of considerable importance. Lynn develops and discusses a series of specific hypotheses regarding parental and sex-role identification. Ellis suggests several propositions with respect to upward mobility. Both authors believe socialization processes are important determining factors in describing behavior. Although neither author writes directly about these processes, they point to cultural or structural variables that do make a difference in the way one is socialized and in subsequent behavior. Both presentations are systematic; they clearly and concisely spell out a tightly articulated formulation to guide future research in role identification and social mobility.

In the second section, the processes of identification and internalization are presented in two excellent studies. Mussen and Distler and Moulton, et al. report findings that bear directly on the processes of interaction, power relations, and affectional relations (nurturance). Each study admirably demonstrates that certain consequences such as sex-typing and guilt or conscience are functions of particular combinations of interaction between child and parents. Both studies support the notion that interaction, nurturance, and power relations must be operative if identification is to occur. Although each study is concerned with only one or two dependent variables, it seems clear that if these processes lead to the internalization of a particular personality trait with behavioral consequences, the same processes should be generally operative for the internalization of other traits, such as values, attitudes, and role behavior.

Part III describes social structural factors that can have an effect upon the fundamental conditions of the identification and socialization processes. Barry, Bacon, and Child utilize ethnographic reports of 110 cultures to point out large sex differences in socialization associated with the type of economy and the customs that encourage large family systems. From these generalizations, they attempt to analyze sex differences in socialization in our society.

Turner, in a similar but much more specific vein, provides data that show it is the *nature* of the father's occupation, rather than his social class position as such, that influences the level of achievement motivation in sons. To be sure, other aspects of socialization are affected by social class position, but Turner's article is an example of well executed research demonstrating that social structural variables do have an impact on the consequences of socialization. Still another example of how social structure affects interpersonal relations is provided in Levanthal's study of family composition and the influence that brothers and sisters have in determining sex-role behavior. There are alternative explanations to those found by Levanthal, but what should be noted is that interaction patterns within one's primary group do have an impact on socialization, and whether one's siblings are older or younger, male or female, makes a difference in the way one is socialized.

Finally, Part IV deals with resocialization. Adamek and Dager use data on semi-delinquent girls from a closed institution to identify the processes which facilitate change in personality. The article is primarily intended to describe the interactional as well as the formal mechanisms utilized to facilitate the girls' identification with the institution and persons within the institution, and the consequent changes that occurred in many of the girls.

Each of the readings incorporates references which the reader should pursue for more detailed knowledge of socialization. Other works which will benefit the reader are listed below.

Suggested Reading

Child, I. L. 1954. Socialization. In G. Lindzey (ed.), *Handbook of social psychology*, vol. 2. Cambridge, Mass.: Addison-Wesley. Pp. 655–92.

Clausen, J. A. (ed.) 1968. *Socialization and society.* Boston: Little, Brown.

Dager, E. Z. 1964. Socialization and personality development in the child. In H. T. Christensen (ed.), *Handbook of marriage and the family.* Chicago: Rand McNally. Pp. 740–81.

Goslin, D. A. (ed.) 1969. *Handbook of socialization theory and research.* Chicago: Rand McNally.

Hoffman, M. L., and Lois W. Hoffman. 1964. *Review of child development research*, vols. 1 and 2. New York: Russell Sage Foundation.

Moore, W. E. 1960. Theories of social change. *American Sociological Review* 25, no. 6: 810–18.

Parsons, T., and R. F. Bales. 1955. *Family, socialization and interaction process.* Glencoe, Ill.: The Free Press.

Sears, R. R.; Lucy Rau; and R. Alpert. 1965. *Identification and child rearing.* Stanford, Cal.: Stanford University Press.

Sewell, W. H. 1963. Some recent developments in socialization theory and research. *The Annals of the American Academy of Political and Social Science* 349: 163–81.

Winch, R. F. 1962. *Identification and its familial determinants.* Indianapolis: Bobbs-Merrill.

Wrong, D. H. 1961. The oversocialized conception of man in modern sociology. *American Sociological Review* 26, no. 2: 183–93.

Contents

I

Socialization
and Social Control

1

Social Control and Self-Regulation

S. F. NADEL

I

No one will quarrel with the assertion that social existence is controlled existence, for we all accept a certain basic assumption about human nature—namely, that without some constraint of individual leanings the coordination of action and regularity of conduct which turn a human aggregation into a society could not materialize. It is thus true to say that "the concept of social control brings us to the focus of sociology and its perpetual problem—the relation of the social order and the individual being, the relation of the unit and the whole."[1]

The question arises where this control resides. Clearly, the social order as such already constrains or controls; institutions, mores, patterned relationships, and all the other constituents of social existence prescribe modes of thought and action and hence canalize and curb individual leanings. In this sense control is simply coterminous with society, and in examining the former we simply describe the latter. Many sociologists choose such a broad interpretation. To quote from MacIver: "A very large part of

S. F. Nadel, "Social Control and Self-Regulation," *Social Forces* 31 (March 1953): 265–73.
[1]R. M. MacIver and Charles Page, *Society* (New York: Rinehart, 1949), p. 137.

sociological literature, *by whatever name* [my italics], treats of social control. . . . To study social control we must seek out the ways in which society patterns and regulates individual behavior. . . ."[2]

Yet the fact that institutions, mores, and so forth, operating as they do upon potentially intractable human material, can maintain themselves and have stability suggests that there must be further controls, safeguarding their continuance. These further controls are, of course, well known. They are exemplified in legal sanctions, in procedures of enforcement, and in any formalized apportionment of rewards and punishments, that is, in all institutions specifically designed to buttress the accepted norms of behaviour and coming into play for no purposes other than appropriate encouragement or restraint. So understood, the social controls no longer simply coincide with social existence but represent a special province within it and a special machinery outside the particular order they are meant to protect.

Anthropologists will tend to adopt this narrower definition, for they would lay that other, more immediate and pervasive control of human nature into their concept of culture or custom. For example, "The social controls found in a culture . . . are a body of customs by which the behaviour of the participants is regulated so that they conform to the culture."[3] This seems the more profitable viewpoint, especially since it brings out the diversity of the processes involved, culture "moulding" or "canalizing" human drives, needs, or desires, while controls reinforce conformity and block deviance.

Viewed in this fashion the anthropological field is rich in instances demonstrating that societies keep their orderliness and cultures, their character even, though controls may be weakly developed or even absent. This suggests, then, that social systems or cultures must in some measure be self-sustaining. The familiar reference to the "force of custom," often taken to be paramount in primitive society, probably always has this implication. But it can be argued, more generally, that no society or culture can be without some elements of self-regulation and that any other

[2]MacIver and Page, *Society,* p. 137.
[3]J. S. Slotkin, *Social Anthropology* (New York: Macmillan, 1950), p. 525.

assumption leads to absurd consequences; for if all cultural modes of thought and action, in order to function adequately, need specific controls, we might well ask what is controlling the controls, and so on *ad infinitum.*

What follows is an attempt to describe and specify the main elements of self-regulation. The first point to be made is that little is gained by adducing the force of custom and tradition, that is, the sheer inertia of habitual behaviour and inherited practices. At least, this force is not a final, irreducible datum.

II

Traditional behaviour, perpetuated through the habituations of long practice, has been numbered among the basic and irreducible types of social action by no less an authority than Max Weber[4]; yet it is doubtful if it can thus stand on its own, at least as regards conduct of any consequence.[5] Rather, traditional or customary behaviour operates reliably only when two other conditions apply and derives its force and apparent self-propulsion from them. Either acting in accordance with tradition (i.e., in accordance with old inherited models) is as such considered desirable and good; or, this way of acting happens also to be safe, known routine. In the first case the traditional action is also value-oriented, being indeed short-lived without this support, as is instanced by changing fashions and fads. In the second case the custom remains such because its routinized procedure affords maximum success with least risk. It is, I suggest, in these two conditions that we find the true elements of self-regulation.

This conclusion is borne out by a further consideration. It must not be assumed that custom (as now understood) takes care only of the less important features of social life while those relevant or crucial are safeguarded by specific controls. In the

[4]Max Weber, *The Theory of Social and Economic Organization,* trans. by A. M. Henderson and Talcott Parsons (New York: Oxford University Press, 1947), p. 105.

[5]Weber only admits that the "pure type" of traditional behaviour (as of all the other basic modes of action) is rarely met with in concrete situations; there, it will tend to shade over into or overlap with the other types, especially with "value-oriented" action.

kind of society anthropologists mostly study, this is certainly not true, custom and tradition governing a wide field of conduct and, within it, activities of great relevance. Indeed, it can be shown that in primitive societies the specific controls, far from being indispensable in safeguarding important activities, tend to be weakest in their case. In other words, any activity which is socially important may by this very fact already be protected from deviance or neglect.

There is nothing surprising or paradoxical in this assertion once we are clear on what we mean by "social importance." There are various criteria for its assessment, of which two are relevant in this context. First, an important social activity is stated to be such by the actors; the criterion therefore lies in the value judgments and convictions of the people we study. Secondly, from the observer's point of view, the importance of any social activity is established by its focal position among all the other social activities; more precisely, any activity is important to the extent to which a series of others depend on it, in a practical and instrumental sense, being incapable of achievement without the focal activity or impeded by any variation (through neglect or disregard) in the latter. This nexus in turn rests on the multivalence of social activities. By this term I mean, briefly, the capacity of any activity (to the extent to which it is focal) to serve also ends or interests other than the one for which it is explicitly or primarily designed. Examples will presently be quoted.[6]

As regards the first criterion of importance, I shall attempt to show that convictions about values have sufficient force to sustain and direct behaviour with no aid other than that implied in the second criterion. And as regards this, it includes self-regulation by definition; for the more focal any mode of behaviour, the more strongly it is rendered invariant by the aggregate pressure of all the other activities and interests dependent on

---

[6]The "multivalence" of social activities has been described in various terms. Malinowski used to speak in a similar context of "amalgamation of functions." Recently Firth referred to the "concern" which an "action or relation has for all other elements in the social system in which it appears"; see Raymond Firth, *Elements of Social Organization* (London: Watts, 1951), p. 35. See also S. F. Nadel, *Foundations of Social Anthropology* (London: Cohen and West, 1951), pp. 123–24, 137–38.

it—lest indeed social life, or a wide area within it, become dislocated. Adherence to the prescribed (and important) norm of action is thus, once more, adherence to a safe procedure, both for the society at large and for the individual actor.

That the two supports of self-regulation—notions of value and instrumental nexus—hang together has already been suggested. They can in fact be regarded as complementary, for if values imply positive guidance for action, the effect of the instrumental nexus is to impede deviance from given courses of action. It will be more convenient to begin with the discussion of the latter.

III

In prototype form, the instrumental nexus appears also in single activities; for any mode of action which is an appropriate means to a given end tends to become routinized and self-maintaining for that reason. This principle (exemplified already in the psychological "law of effect" governing elementary learning processes) is essentially one of economy, in effort and trial-and-error; and the most convincing instances in social life probably come from the field of technology and economics in general. But aesthetic and recreational activities are similarly self-regulating, for any artistic style will again be perpetuated as long as it represents an adequate means for its particular end (the desired satisfaction or stimulation). The infrequency of technological invention in primitive societies provides the broadest evidence of this kind. If it be argued that this proves, not the self-maintenance of adequate methods, but a primitive, tradition-bound mentality, which prevents people from exploring new and possibly better procedures, the answer is this: primitive peoples are disinterested only in inventiveness, in experimentation with new techniques, not in innovations as such. Significantly, they have little hesitation in copying (or borrowing) novel methods, that is, in adopting them when they can be seen *in use.* The pull of tradition, then, means in fact reluctance to abandon a safe routine for the risks that go with untried methods.

Why this factor should be more powerful in primitive than in advanced societies we need not discuss. But it must be mentioned that in the former the tenacity of inherited routines, technological or aesthetic, is often reinforced by sanctification. Now this means that the routine is invested with an additional value of sacredness or of desirability in virtue of divine derivation and the like; and this means, further, that the technological or aesthetic task is meant to serve more than one interest. For it is now required to attain its own intrinsic goal as well as conform to religious commands, lest the actors forfeit some expected benefit, imaginary (supernatural protection) or real (the normal fellowship which might be refused to the irreligious). We note that this is already a first instance of that more far-reaching self-regulation which we derived from the interdependence of diverse social activities and from multivalence or focal position.

IV

Any mode of behaviour operating also as a *diacritical sign* (i.e., a differentiating sign or symbol) is multivalent to a simple degree. Thus customs of dress, eating habits, style of residence, or manners of speech, apart from attaining their intrinsic ends (protection of the body, satiation of hunger, shelter, communication), will often also indicate a person's social status, group or class membership, and generally his social relationship with others. The continuance of these indicative modes of behaviour is thus reinforced by the importance of the state of affairs they indicate. Or, in terms of individual behaviour, individuals will keep up a certain dialect, manner of dress, and so forth, in order to evince their status and group membership and, implicitly, to qualify for the benefits that go with them.

We note that the additional valence of the activities in question attaches to their form or style, not to the efficiency with which they are performed and attain their intrinsic ends. In other instances it is the latter which has the double valence, in the sense that efficiency in the performance of one activity becomes a qualification for participation in a second, desired one. Among the Nupe of West Africa, for example, a man whose sons are guilty of a serious misdemeanour cannot hope to be appointed to a rank and title[7]; among a certain Nuba tribe in the Sudan a candidate for shaman priestship will be unsuccessful if he happens to be a lazy or unsuccessful farmer.[8] We might here, briefly, speak of an incentive or premium meant to ensure the socially approved conduct.

Examples of this kind can easily be multiplied. But it is important to emphasize that the incentive is incidental, not specific, and that the rewarding achievement is such—a premium—only among other things. If it were not so, we should be dealing with a specific machinery of control, not with features of self-regulation. Nupe society is not otherwise concerned with the success of parental discipline (save in approving of it), and the bestowal of ranks and titles implies other, more relevant, qualifications besides; the Nuba tribe does not reward good farmers and punish bad ones, and again expects would-be shamans to give more substantial proof of their eligibility. All that happens is that parental discipline or diligent farming is linked with the other desired achievements, failures in the former reducing the chances of the latter. Differently expressed, deviations from the socially approved conduct are *penalized* (not punished). The step from one to the other, though narrow, is unmistakable. We need only think of the exclusion from sacramental offices of sinners or of the loss of civil rights threatening political criminals.

It is clear that the efficacy of such linked incentives requires a closely geared social system. In our examples the public standards of conduct are affected only because every man is both a family head and a potential rank-holder, a farmer and a possible candidate for priestship. The linkage itself presupposes that rank and priestship are conceived sufficiently broadly for the specialized qualifications to be combined with other, extraneous ones. In more general terms, the regulative effects must vary inversely with the separation of social roles, with the specialization of offices and tasks, and, implicitly, with the size of groups (since only small groups can function adequately without considerable internal differentiation). It is precisely the small scale and lack of internal differentiation which characterize the societies we com-

---

[7]S. F. Nadel, *A Black Byzantium* (London: Oxford University Press, 1942), p. 64.
  [8]S. F. Nadel, *The Nuba* (London: Oxford University Press, 1947), p. 442.

monly call primitive and hence enable them to lean more heavily on such machinery of self-regulation.[9]

Its effects may be rendered both more pervasive and more unspecific, consisting in general complications and obstacles facing any person who would depart from the accepted norm. The premium, then, lies merely in the smoothly functioning, normal course of events individuals expect to encounter; the penalty, in normality dislocated and expectations disappointed. Some of the most crucial norms of conduct in primitive societies, such as exogamy or incest taboos, are often regulated by no more specific sanctions, secular or religious, yet are adhered to with great strictness.

Consider for example, a society, patrilineally organized, where marriage is prohibited between aganatic kin, is contracted by the payment of brideprice, and entails specific duties towards the offspring on the part of both father's and mother's kin. If any man married in disregard of the first rule, the others would fail to work also. The brideprice would have to be paid within the same descent group, while in the people's conception it is a payment suitable only between such groups, being meant (among other things) to indemnify the bride's group for the loss of her prospective progeny. The offspring of such an irregular union would forfeit the double assistance from two kin groups since the father's and mother's kin now coincide, and would be less advantageously placed than the offspring of customary marriages. And there would be various other, minor but no less confusing, complications; for example, rules of avoidance (obligatory towards in-laws) and intimacy (towards blood relations) would now apply to the same people. In short, one breach of routine disrupts routine all round, and the individual is faced with a wide loss of social bearings.

It has been suggested that this type of marriage enables kinship affiliations to be extended beyond the single descent group and thus creates additional bonds consolidating an otherwise segmented society.[10] This, then, is one of the multivalences

[9]Highly complex societies, too, exploit it whenever they are organized on "totalitarian" lines, e.g., when social promotion of any kind is impossible unless the candidate professes the "right" kind of religion of political conviction or lives according to approved standards of morality.

[10]E. E. Evans-Pritchard, *The Nuer* (Oxford: Clarendon Press, 1940), p. 225.

underlying the chain of effects just described: the institution of marriage, over and above regulating sex relations and procreation, also serves that other end, the strengthening of social solidarity. It is doubtful if the actors themselves think, or think clearly, in terms of this ulterior objective (or function). Yet if they are not capable of assessing this widest instrumental nexus, they are aware of the multiple consequences threatening them personally, and act from this knowledge.

This is only a restatement, from the actors' standpoint, of the point made before, that the crucial importance (or focal position) of any mode of action also protects it from deviation. Here, too, the character of self-regulation is most clearly marked. For consider that in the specific controls the disabilities (or sanctions) imposed upon the transgressor are mostly extrinsic to his mode of conduct, leaving the success of the latter unaffected. An adulterer, for example, though he may have to face flogging, a fine, or imprisonment, will have attained the satisfaction sought in the criminal act. In the instances here considered the penalty is intrinsic, lying in the incapacity of the criminal act to provide the expected satisfaction: the unorthodox marriage is simply an unsuccessful marriage judged by all the expectations it normally fulfills.

Quite often this notion of self-regulation by ill-success finds explicit expression. The potential transgressor will merely be warned of the frustrating and self-negating consequences of such-and-such a mode of action. The Navaho Indian, for example, "never appeals to abstract morality or to adherence to divine principles. He stresses mainly practical consequences: 'If you don't tell the truth, your fellows won't trust you and you'll shame your relatives. You'll never get along in the world that way'."[11] At least, statements of this kind will appear couched in terms of imagined, supernatural guarantees. Thus in a Nuba tribe incestuous marriages are said to remain barren, and the people would add, "Since one marries for the sake of children no one would break the marriage rules."[12] The Tikopia hold similar views and

[11]Clyde Kluckhohn and Dorothea Leighton, *The Navaho* (Cambridge, Mass.: Harvard University Press, 1946), p. 218.
[12]Nadel, *The Nuba*, p. 430.

in fact explicitly state that incestuous marriages are doomed to failure or ill-success.[13] And proverbially there is the curse on ill-gotten gains.

We may finally consider the extreme case, when the loss of social bearings is very nearly complete. Here the transgressor is practically excluded from all normal expectations, left without a niche, and relegated to the role of a misfit. In primitive societies it is often unheard of for a man or woman to remain unmarried. Now this phrase "unheard of" indicates the pressure of the multiple consequences: the bachelor could reach no position of responsibility or authority; his economic pursuits would be seriously hampered in a society where the family is the main source of cooperative labour; he might have no one to look after him in sickness or old age; and no one even to bury him or perform the rites of the dead. In the Nuba society mentioned before, dissolution of marriage, though not unheard of, is considered most undesirable and in conflict with tradition. In practice this means that the woman who leaves her husband can never enjoy normal life: her children would not be hers; she forfeits the support of her own kin; and she would die without the customary ceremonial.

Let me stress that these consequences still represent only ill-success in the business of living, as it were, not genuine sanctions—disabilities specifically inflicted. The culprits merely suffer failures which, in a society so-and-so constituted, cannot be avoided once the rules are broken. There is no intentional discrimination against the offenders *qua* offenders; nor is there any thought of a stigma imposed on them (say, that of "living in sin") and ostracism because of this. Rather, as we shall see, stigmatization is on the whole alien to primitive societies.

V

Whenever we spoke above of desired, approved, good actions or their opposites we were, of course, already referring to values. Indeed, this concept, like that of social control, can be

[13]Raymond Firth, *We, the Tikopia* (New York: American Book Company, 1936), p. 334.

given so wide a connotation that it becomes coextensive with social existence or social behaviour. For since the latter is, by definition, regular and aimful behaviour, thus implying consistent choices between possible courses of action, social life in its entirety might be said to express or implement preferences and idiosyncrasies, notions of worthwhileness and undesirability, in short, values. This view is expressed, for example, by Lasswell and Kaplan: "A value is a desired event—a goal event"; "Conduct is goal-directed and hence implicates values."[14]

It is more profitable, however, to restrict the concept somewhat, in this sense. It shall be understood to refer to worthwhileness of a non-trivial kind (excluding, for example, table manners, fashions of dress, etc.); it shall not be coterminous with practical utility (e.g., of tools, technological procedures) but bear on more autonomous forms of worthwhileness (e.g., things morally good or aesthetically desirable); it shall refer to classes of objects (things, events, states of affairs desired or disdained), not to individual ones, so that it indicates maxims of action, not *ad hoc* preferences; and the former shall be ideologically founded, i.e., capable of being expressed by the actors in generalized assertions on right and wrong and the like.

It is clear and hardly worth saying that the specific controls found in any society inevitably imply values and normally refer to values widely accepted. What is important is that controls cannot ever be wholly effective unless they endorse what most people hold desirable (or value), which point is amply illustrated by the difficulties of enforcing laws no one believes in or of maintaining a hated regime. Even societies relying on machineries of control, then, must rely also on values simply held. Ultimately, the social norm has power inasmuch as it is internalized, that is, inasmuch as the public assertions on right and wrong are also the private convictions of individuals. In the language of psychoanalysis, the commands made on behalf of the society are absorbed in the Super-Ego.

We may for the moment disregard the processes whereby the Super-Ego is built up, through verbal instruction and the impact

---

[14]Harold D. Lasswell and Abraham Kaplan, *Power and Society* (New Haven: Yale University Press, 1950), pp. 16, 240.

of models for acting. Nor need we emphasize again that in primitive societies it seems sufficiently powerful to determine conduct unaided by extraneous controls. But, as previously suggested, even where there are controls, their chain ends at some point; and here values simply held, internalized, will be the final pivots of desired conduct. In that sphere the observer can only state that, say, matrimonial sanctity or the observance of exogamy are held to be "right" or "good" and deviations from the norm, wrong or evil.

Sanctification will often obscure this self-reliance, deriving the final values from divine ordinances or some superhuman authority. Perhaps the religious guise, reducing as it does the absoluteness of the moral or social norm to quasi-human acts of will or providence, invests the norm with greater persuasiveness; at least, the acceptance of ultimate principles is moved back a further stage and joined to that other ultimate conception of an ordered universe. But in primitive societies this theological sophistication is often absent. There is no conception of deities as law givers; rather, they are merely the guardians and exponents of the moral principles. If they punish or reward they do so only because they are themselves subject to the given doctrine of good and evil. As Firth points out for the Tikopia, "The spirits, just as men, respond to a norm of conduct of an external character. The moral law exists in the absolute, independent of the gods."[15] Indeed, the supreme deity may be altogether aloof from all moral concerns, while minor deities, spirits, or other mystic forces, would aid or hinder human action regardless of moral principles. Their influences are needed only to explain why "good" actions may fail and "evil" ones triumph, and hence to serve as a foil for the self-reliance of the accepted values. Furthermore, sanctification as such, making any object or action sacred, holy, or mystically "right," merely adds another notion of worthwhileness, no less final than the simple "good."

Yet even where supernatural sanctions are accepted, they clearly cannot be simply aligned with secular social controls. That punishment and reward will materialize, administered perhaps by an omniscient deity, is a question of faith, not of verifiable

[15]Firth, *We, the Tikopia*, p. 335.

consequences; and this conviction is much closer to the internalized dictates of conscience than to the anticipation of public correctives or appraisals. Nor is it rare for the supernatural sanctions to be so conceived that they are entirely reduced to appeals to conscience. Among the Nuba tribes infringements of clan taboos or exogamy are sometimes believed to be punished with leprosy, which may unpredictably befall any descendant of the culprit. The potential sinner, then, will be restrained by the fear of bringing suffering and disgrace upon someone he does not even know, that is, by a further emphasis on the evilness of his deed.

In one respect belief in supernatural punishment differs sharply from internalized values. Any deed inviting the former, any sin, that is, can usually be expiated, the system of beliefs defining the sin also showing the procedure for regaining purity. But disregard of the dictates of conscience entails guilt, the awareness of which cannot be wiped out by established procedures. The conflict thus engendered must be resolved or borne by the individual alone and may well leave only escape into neurosis or suicide.[16] I do not know and can hardly imagine a society which relies exclusively on internalized commands and their correlate, guilt. That guilt is so often made translatable into sin reflects, I suggest, this risk—which no society can face—of denying to culprits all chances of expiation.

VI

We may, in the same light, assess the merits and demerits of self-regulation by "multiple consequences." Consider that any sanction proper (disregarding the extreme penalties of death, life imprisonment, and perhaps expulsion) limits the consequences of

---

[16]Malinowski quotes several examples of suicide committed in consequence of such overwhelming awareness of guilt—"as means of escape from situations without issue"; see his *Crime and Custom* (New York: Harcourt, Brace, 1926), pp. 94ff. Though these examples refer to a guilt reinforced by shame, i.e., brought into the open by direct or public accusation, this does not detract from the crucial guilt motive.

the crime to a single event, the punishment, and afterwards offers the culprit a new chance. But the obstacles and hardships the offender creates for himself when committing an unpunishable offense cannot be cut short by any single act of atonement. Though they may involve less physical suffering, they are more hopeless since there is no way of repairing that total loss of social bearings. The more widely a society relies on the automatic efficacy of this threat, the more severely are offenders imprisoned in their own actions. I know of no society completely commited to this method of self-regulation; but it is sufficiently powerful in some primitive groups to account for self-exile or even that ultimate means of escape, suicide.

Primitive societies are in this respect in a dilemma. As I have suggested, it is their smallness, low internal differentiation, and closely knit organization which afford the possibilities of far-reaching self-regulation; and it is precisely societies of this kind which are weakened most seriously by the loss of members. The adoption of specific mechanisms of control, therefore, apart from corresponding to the requirements of a less closely geared social system, also represents a loophole in a social system too rigidly and permanently penalizing transgression.

The underlying assumption, that primitive societies are aware of this risk and hence in some measure concerned with rehabilitating offenders, is easily proved. It is borne out by the widespread treatment of homicide almost as a "civil" offense, so that even murderers can, after payment of *wergeld* or similar compensations, resume their normal place in the community. Frequently too there are formalized procedures of reconciliation after the punishment of torts, meant to "cleanse the hearts of anger" and to accentuate the fact that the transgression has been disposed of. Similarly, primitive societies make little use of any lasting stigma or ostracism. In no society is it altogether avoidable that the disgrace of a particular transgression should follow the culprit through life and overshadow all his contacts with his fellow men. But there can be no doubt that it is the advanced rather than the primitive society which tends to exploit this effect in consciously creating the outcast or his milder version, the *déclassé* individual. If in certain primitive groups stigmatization does occur, this is only part of another dilemma: for the same society would in other ways show its desire to rehabilitate offenders.[17]

VII

It will perhaps be argued that I could attribute such importance to self-regulation and especially to values simply held only because I neglected two crucial and ubiquitous controls—the diffuse sanctions implied in public criticism, shame or ridicule, and the institutionalized procedures of education. My answer would be that the two controls not only safeguard but also presuppose values and hence represent, not so much controls acting from outside upon the desired conduct, as phases in a circular process whereby values engender conduct and conduct reinforces values.

Voiced disapproval, of any kind or mood, may of course be merely a sign foreshadowing more compelling consequences (i.e., some concrete penalization, some loss, more or less severe, of normal chances). Disregarding this eventuality, the disturbing psychological effects of the disapproval, without which it would not be a sanction, presuppose that it cannot be evaded or disregarded. If, say, the shamefulness of adultery is not a matter of general agreement, the adulterer (assuming he is not punished in any other way) will always find some supporters among the public and be able to heed their approval rather than the disapproval of others. Above all, if he does not himself endorse the criticism, even tacitly or subconsciously, he can simply set it aside as irrelevant. In other words, blame, ridicule, or holding up to shame are controls only if they express commonly accepted values and correspond to the promptings of the Super-Ego. Admittedly, they also bring these promptings into the open; but this only means that they render them more acute. Indeed, it might be said that the strongest of these diffuse sanctions, shame,

[17]Thus in the Trobriands, where the breach of exogamy is followed by ostracism (which may drive the culprits to suicide), blood revenge is mostly replaced by compensation (a "peacemaking price"). Malinowski, *Crime and Custom*, pp. 80, 115.

derives its very strength from the fact that it is an "exposure"—of inadequacies privately felt.[18]

As regards education, it is a truism to say that its widest efficacy (ignoring purely technical skills) lies in the inculcation of lasting attitudes and viewpoints, that is, of values subsequently to be simply held and followed. Without this, its force of control would be restricted to the actual period of tuition, when the educator employs rewards and punishment and other means of coercion; nor could there be any reason why a child taught a particular way of behaving should, as an adult, hand on this knowledge to his offspring, thus perpetuating the social order. Education, then, as I see it, merely provides occasions for self-regulation to emerge or re-emerge.

Needless to say, it is not the only such occasion. The notions of worthwhileness taught in family or school are reinforced in various ways throughout life—by religious doctrine, by the topics of art or legends, and by the symbolic dramatizations of ritual. But here it is difficult to distinguish between occasions and consequences or, if we call the former "controls," between these and the things controlled. The methods of education, the content of art, religious beliefs, though they demonstrate and enjoin precepts for conduct, are themselves forms of conduct and perpetuated only because they follow from these very precepts. We have, in the last resort, merely multiple instances of a given system of values, irreducible to any further regulative machinery save that circular process mentioned before, which seems inherent in any value system of real efficacy. The circularity goes even further; for any public act in harmony with the obtaining values becomes in some degree a model exhibiting their validity, and so adds to their efficacy. Whenever a person observes, say, exogamy or pursues blood revenge as demanded by the social norm, he not only executes a prescribed procedure but adds to the instances demonstrating that this procedure is indeed valid, which addition is as much a reinforcement of the moral values as is their explicit assertion or teaching.

For this widest circularity we find a physical model in what

[18]Erik H. Erikson, *Childhood and Society* (New York: W. W. Norton, 1950), p. 223.

are now known as "feed-back" systems.[19] Taking the whole society to be the relevant system, any "output" of the intended kind—any conduct in accordance with the social norm—is partly returned as "input," i.e., as information sustaining further action of that character. The self-regulation implied in "linked incentives" and "multiple consequences" represents the exact counterpart. If the efficacy of values corresponds to a "positive feed-back," the other types of self-regulation correspond to "negative feed-back," controlling output through signalling errors—the errors being the forms of deviant conduct whose penalizing consequences force action back into the intended channels.

It will be seen, further, that guidance through values and penalization must operate consistently if the social order is to be maintained. The positive precepts of worthwhileness will normally reduce experimentation with unorthodox conduct. Yet if the latter does occur and fails to carry its own penalty, the underlying values will inevitably be weakened. This mutual agreement probably represents the most vulnerable area in any social system, for here theoretical convictions and practical experience must teach the same lesson. The frequent cry of morality collapsing nearly always refers to a situation where disregard for conduct taught and enjoined is no longer penalized through being demonstrably unsuccessful. The social order, if it is to survive, must then be refashioned, with values once more consistent with practical experience.[20]

We may add, finally, that the specific controls are equally fitted into the circularity of value systems. For the controls both follow from the value system and demonstrate it, since the punishments and rewards bestowed by societies are normally public acts. That circle is broken only when rulers, judges, legislators or, for that matter, teachers and moralists apply or preach a doctrine in which they themselves do not believe. They

[19]See F. C. S. Northrop, ed., *Ideological Differences and the World Order* (New Haven: Yale University Press, 1949), p. 420; and Norbert Wiener, *Cybernetics* (Cambridge, Mass.: Technology Press, 1948), pp. 13, 54, 114–15.

[20]Weber's and Tawney's familiar studies relating the Reformation to the rise of capitalism demonstrate such a process of reconstituted consistency, between a new rewarding economic practice and a value system hitherto deprecating wealth and material success.

then stand outside the value system they wish to maintain, whoever they may be—a conquering minority enforcing laws fit for the masses, a group of Supermen *a la* Neitzsche, claiming to be "beyond good and evil," or a cynical *elite a la* Pareto or Sorel.[21] Here the question, "what is controlling the controls?" makes sense: the answer is—self-interest and calculations of political expediency. And here, if you like, we touch upon social controls in purest form, exercised from outside and unobscured as well as unaided by any self-regulation.

[21]Cf. Karl Mannheim's summing up of Fascist ideology: "The superior person, the leader, knows that all political and historical ideas are myths. He himself is entirely emancipated from them, but he values them . . . because they . . . stimulate enthusiastic feelings . . . and are the only forces that lead to [the desired] political activity." *Ideology and Utopia* (New York: Harcourt, Brace, 1936), pp. 122–23.

II

Socialization Theory and Research

A. Theory

2

The Choice of Variables
in the Study of Socialization

ELEANOR E. MACCOBY

Perhaps the greatest change that has occurred in the field of child development in the past 15 years has been the increasing emphasis on socialization. The change may be traced by comparing the more traditional textbooks with recent ones. The scholarly child psychology text by Munn (16),* for example, does not bring up the topic of parent-child interaction until the 16th chapter, and here devotes only eight pages to a topic called "environmental influences and personality," a heading under which he presents all that the book has to say on "mothering," on Freudian theory of developmental stages, on ordinal position—in fact, on socialization in general. Contrast this with a book such as Watson's

Eleanor E. Maccoby, "The Choice of Variables in the Study of Socialization," *Sociometry* 24 (1961): 357–71.

This article is a composite of two papers, one delivered at the Berkeley Conference on Personality Development in Childhood in April, 1960, and the other delivered at the American Psychological Association Meeting in New York in August, 1961.

*The reference list is numbered at the end of the chapter.

(23), in which more than half the book is devoted to a discussion of socialization theory and a detailed consideration of the impressive amounts of research that have recently been done on the subject.

The same increasing emphasis on socialization may be seen in the child-development journals. And, of course, the widespread research interest in this topic has led to the development of several research instruments for the measurement of parental attitudes and behavior. There are the Fels scales (2), developed during the 40s, for the rating of parent behavior; the parent interview schedule developed by Sears and his associates at Harvard and Stanford (21), the parent attitude scales developed by Shoben at U.S.C. (22), and the widely-used Parent Attitude Research Instrument scales developed at the National Institutes of Health by Schaeffer and Bell (20), to mention only a few. Each investigator, when he sat down to make a first draft of his rating scale or interview schedule or attitude scale items, had to ask himself the question: What shall I measure? What are the important variables in parental behavior that ought to make a difference in the development of the child? The process of selecting and defining variables is, of course, the very heart of theory-making. There are as many possible variables as there are ideas about what causes what in human development. I cannot attempt here to give any sort of roster of variables; the task would be too great and might not prove very useful. I simply want to point out some of the major classes of variables that have been used and give a little of the history of the reasons why we have chosen to measure these things and not others and perhaps point to a few ways in which we could clarify the meaning of the dimension we are using.

Let us start with the traditional child psychologist, with his interests in motor development, emotional development, intelligence, concept formation, and personality development, all grounded in traditional principles of learning and maturation. He may look upon the current work in socialization with a jaundiced eye and inquire what the excitement is all about. He may feel that he has actually been studying socialization for years without calling it by this name. He might put his question this way: If it is true that socialization is the process of transmitting culture from one generation to another, and that the child acquires the modes of behavior prescribed by his culture through the process of learning, then how is the study of socialization any different from the study of learning itself? One might reply that in socialization studies, we study not only the child as learner but the parent as teacher. But a skeptic might still wonder how much difference this actually makes. For example, laboratory studies of learning have demonstrated that behavior which is followed by reward will be strengthened, and its probability of recurrence will be increased. Now, if a student of socialization does a study of dependency, and discovers that parents who reward their children for dependency have more dependent children, has he really found out anything that we didn't know already?

In my opinion, it *is* valuable to carry out at the human level studies which attempt to employ the standard variables that have grown out of laboratory study on learning, where most of the work has been done on subhuman species. But, in the process of applying such variables to socialization studies, the variables almost perforce undergo certain modifications and elaborations, with the result that translating traditional behavior theory variables into the socialization setting sometimes results in the addition of something new, and the possibility of getting new kinds of principles.

Let me give an example. Suppose we wanted to study the effects of a particular schedule of reward. What do we mean by reward? The traditional approach to reward has been to produce a physiological drive, such as hunger or thirst, through deprivation; and then to reinforce the desired behavior by presenting a drive-relevant reinforcing stimulus. But even in fairly young children, a rapid development of complex motivation occurs, and this changes the nature of the reinforcements to which children will be responsive. B. F. Skinner encountered this fact when he was developing his teaching machines. The early models were devised so as to emit little pieces of chocolate candy whenever a child made the correct response. But it was soon evident that a child progressed through a series of arithmetic or spelling problems just as readily without the candy; in fact, the giving of candy sometimes disrupted the learning process. Skinner, therefore, abandoned the candy rewards, and the current models of his machine rely upon no other reward than the child's interest in doing his work correctly—buttressed, no doubt, by a certain amount of pressure from the teacher and parents. This incident illustrates a major question about the definition of variables: what happens to the variable "amount of reward" when it is translated into situations of teacher-child, or parent-child, interaction? In modern societies, children's physiological drives are regularly and quite fully satisfied and are seldom used as a basis for training. That is, most parents do not let the child get hungry, thirsty, wet, or overtired, and then make the satisfaction of these needs conditional on good behavior. Rather, the rewards used are money, a trip to the zoo, being allowed to stay up for a special TV program, etc. A gift of candy for some children becomes symbolic of affection instead of vice versa. Very commonly, behavior is reinforced simply through the giving of approval, affection, or attention. So the concept "reward," when it refers to the rewards which parents use in socializing their children, is not directly comparable to the concept as it was originally developed in studies of animal learning. Of course, it is not really a new idea to point out that different kinds of organisms are capable of being rewarded by different kinds of things. It is clear enough that there are as many kinds of rewards as there are distinguishable motives, and that both motives and rewards vary between species and within species. But the new idea that has been added in socialization studies is that there may be distinguishable *classes* of rewards which may have different effects. The primary distinction made in studies so far has been between material reward and praise. Material reward covers all instances of giving the child some object or privilege that he wants, conditional upon good behavior. Praise depends to some degree upon the previous establishment of a relationship between the socializing agent and the child, such that the approval of this particular adult is something the child wants. That is, the effectiveness of praise ought to depend upon the identity of the person doing the praising and upon this person's being someone the child loves, fears, or must depend upon for the satisfaction of needs.

The same kind of differentiation of a variable has occurred with respect to punishment. Students of the socialization process have been working under the assumption that not all kinds of aversive events following a child's act will have the same effect. The distinction most commonly made is that between physical punishment and so-called love-oriented discipline, or withdrawal of love. There are other categories of punishment, too, such as withdrawal of privileges and ridicule, which are less interesting than the first two because there are fewer hypotheses about their probable effects. Let us concentrate for a moment on the distinction between physical punishment and withdrawal of love. Physical punishment is easy enough to define, although in rating its frequency and severity, the researcher is always troubled about the problem of how to weigh slaps and shakings in relation to formal spankings. More tricky by far is the matter of defining withdrawal of love. Sears and his associates (ëä) have defined it as any act or statement on the part of the parent that threatens the affectional bond between the parent and child. This would include the mother's turning her back on the child, refusing to speak to him or smile at him or be in the same room with him, saying she doesn't like him when he does disapproved things, etc. The system of classification of techniques of discipline presented by Beverly Allinsmith in her chapter in Miller and Swanson's book, *Inner Conflict and Defense* (1), similarly emphasizes the distinction between "psychological" and "corporal" punishment, but defines psychological discipline somewhat differently. This classification for Allinsmith includes manipulating the child by shaming the child, appealing to his pride or guilt, and expressing disappointment over his misdeeds. But there is another dimension considered in the rating: namely, the amount of emotional control the mother displays in administering her discipline. Thus, if a mother shouts angrily at the child, "I hate you for doing that," Allinsmith would *not* classify this as psychological discipline, while Sears et al. would. But the mother who says calmly and perhaps coldly, "Now, dear, you know I don't like little boys who do that," would be classified as using psychological discipline in both systems. The difference in these two classification systems stems in part from two different views of the nature of the process which gives psychological discipline its effect. Sears et al. view it as a technique which arouses the child's anxiety over whether he is loved and approved of, and thereby elicits efforts on the child's part to regain his parents' approval by conforming, apologizing, or making amends. Allinsmith, on the other hand, emphasizes two things: (a) the *modeling* function of discipline, pointing out that a mother who loses her temper at the same time she is trying to teach the child to control his, will have a child who will do as the mother *does* rather than as she *says;* and (b) the target the child chooses for the aggressive impulses aroused in him as a consequence of punishment. The reasoning here is that the openly angry mother becomes a more legitimate target for the child's counter-aggression. The distinction between the two definitions of the dimension is further brought out when we consider the kinds of findings reported in the studies using them: Sears et al. found that withdrawal of love was associated with high development of conscience, physical punishment with low; Allinsmith found that psychological discipline, as she defined it, was associated with *indirect* fantasy expressions of aggression in the children they studied, corporal punishment with *direct* expression of aggression. All this illustrates the fact that fairly subtle differences in the definition of a dimension can affect the nature of child behavior that can be predicted from it. But more importantly, both these studies illustrate that when we attempted to take over the variable "punishment" from the learning laboratories, we found it necessary to subdivide and differentiate the variable and gained predictive power by doing so.

I have been attempting to cite ways in which I think that socialization studies have improved upon some of the standard variables employed in laboratory studies. There are instances, alas, in which we have not taken note of the differences which exist between the laboratory and the standard socialization settings, and thus have failed to identify and make use of some potentially promising variables. For example, in laboratory studies, we can take it for granted that the experimenter is there during training sessions, administering either reinforcements or aversive stimuli in some orderly relationship to the subject's responses. In the parent-child relationship, the parent is by no means always functioning as a trainer, and parents differ greatly in the degree to which they do so. Some parents keep track quite continuously of what the child is doing, and engage in a constant flow of interaction, both verbal and nonverbal, with the child. Other parents, for a substantial portion of the time they are with their children, are bored, busy, withdrawn, intoxicated, watching television, or subject to some other state or activity which precludes their responding to the child unless he becomes very insistent. In such a household the children are, of course, in a very different learning situation than children growing up with more wholly attentive parents. I think the sheer amount of interaction may in some cases be a more important variable for predicting characteristics of the child than the nature of the interaction that does occur. Let me give an example. In a study Dr. Lucy Rau and I are now doing at Stanford, we have selected groups of children who show discrepancies in their intellectual abilities. That is, we have one group of children who are good at verbal tasks but poor at number, another group who are good at spatial tasks but poor at verbal, etc. One of our students, Mrs. Bing, has interviewed the mothers of the children, and has also conducted some observation sessions in which the mother presents achievement tasks to the child while the observer records the kind and amount of the mother's involvement with the child's work. Mrs. Bing has found that it is the *amount,* rather than the *kind,* of mother-child interaction that best predicts what the child's pattern of intellectual skills will be. That is, the mothers of the highly verbal children use more praise, but also more criticism, than do the mothers of equally bright children whose area of special skill is non-verbal. Their total level of interaction with the child is greater, and this interaction includes the administration of what we would regard as aversive stimuli as well as reinforcements. The variable "amount of interaction" emerged in our factor analysis of the scales in the *Patterns of Child Rearing* study (21)—we titled this variable "responsible child-rearing orientation" for lack of a better name, but we never made much use of the variable because it did not fit in with the theoretical formulation of our study. But I suspect that for any future work in which we are trying to predict such things as the child's cognitive maturity level or his achievement motivation, we may find that this variable is a better predictor than the less global variables (such as amount of praise) that we have been relying on up till now.

So far, I have been discussing the process of translating variables from laboratory studies of learning to the socialization setting, and have pointed out that we have been successful in employing such variables as reward and punishment, but that in the process of using these variables, we have found useful ways of subdividing them. Let us consider the theoretical meaning of the elaborations of these variables that have occurred.

When we make the distinction between material reward and praise, and the distinction between love-oriented punishment and punishment that depends for its effect upon producing direct physical pain, we are really taking note of the fact that the effect of discipline, and in fact the very nature of the discipline that is possible to use with a child, depends upon the history of the relationship that has been developed between the child and the person who is training him. And here is a new class of variables that socialization studies have added to the list of variables derived from classical studies of learning. In laboratory studies of learning, it has not been found necessary (at least until very recently) to ask whether the experimental subject loved or hated the machine that was emitting pellets of food and drops of water, or whether the characteristics of the machine or person presenting the rewards made any difference in the effectiveness of the reinforcement. Socialization studies, on the other hand, have found the identity of the socializing agent, and certain of his personality characteristics, to be important.

The emphasis on the importance of the relationship between trainer and learner came, of course, out of psychodynamic theories of personality development. Learning theory and psychoanalytic theory differ, I think, with respect to what they believe the basic nature of the socialization process is. This is an oversimplification, but I believe it would be reasonably accurate to say that a learning theorist would regard socialization as a learning process in which certain actions of the child's are selected out by virtue of reinforcement, others tried and dropped because they are in some way punished or nonreinforced. The parents have a primary role in administering the rewards and punishments for the child's actions, although they do not necessarily do this deliberately and consciously as a teaching effort. And, of course, there are other sources of reward and punishment than the parents' reactions which will help to determine what behavior the child retains.

The psychoanalytic approach, on the other hand, would emphasize not the detailed learning of specific actions on the basis of their outcome, but the providing of conditions which will motivate the child to take on spontaneously the socialized behavior the parent wants him to have. The terms introjection, internalization, learning through role-playing, and identification have been used in this connection; they all refer to the child's tendency to copy, to take on as his own, the behavior, attitudes, and values of the significant people in his life, even when the socializing agents have not said "that's a good boy" or given him a piece of candy for performing these acts or holding these values. I will not go into the controversy concerning which so much has been written as to whether the child is more likely to identify with the person who is powerful and feared or with the person who is loved; nor will I discuss the several thoughtful efforts by personality theorists to reconcile the two points of view. The only important point for our consideration here is that the psychoanalytic view of socialization has led to an exploration of such variables as the warmth or hostility of the socializing agent toward the child.

There can be no doubt that measures of the warmth of the parent-child relationship have turned out to be enormously useful in socialization studies, in a number of ways. In some studies, warmth has been found to have a direct relationship to some dependent variable. For example, McCord and McCord (14) have found that warmth in fathers was associated with low crime rate in sons. In other studies, warmth has turned out to be a useful crosscutting variable which interacts with other variables in such a way that other variables only begin to show their effects when the sample is first subdivided into groups differing in parental warmth. For example, in the *Patterns of Child Rearing* study, Sears et al. (21) found that withdrawal of love is associated with rapid development of conscience, but only if this technique is employed by a warm mother; also that punishment for toilet accidents disrupts the toilet-training process, but that the greatest disruption occurs if punishment is administered by a cold mother.

Warmth also occupies a central role in socialization studies in its relationship to other measures of child-training variables. There have been, to my knowledge, three factor analyses carried out on sets of socialization variables. One of these was on the Fels parent behavior rating scales (18), one on the PARI (27), and one on the dimensions employed by Sears et al. in the *Patterns* study (21). In the latter two, warmth emerged as a fairly clear factor. In the first, there were two factors, one called "concern for the child" and the other called "parent-child harmony," which taken together are probably close to what is meant by warmth in the other two studies. It is clear, then, that both in terms of its predictive value for the child's behavior and its central place among the other interrelated child-training variables, warmth is a variable to be taken seriously. Why is it so important? I have already pointed out why the psychodynamic theorists believe it to be so—because of its role in producing identification. But the laboratory learning theorists can acknowledge its importance for another very simple reason. Before a parent can socialize a child, he must have established a relationship with the child such that the child will stay in the vicinity of the parent and orient himself toward the parent. A warm parent keeps the child responsive to his directions by providing an atmosphere in which the child has continuous expectations that good things will happen to him if he stays near his parent and responds to his parent's wishes. Fear of punishment can also make the child attentive to the parent, of course, but it establishes as well the conflicting motivation to escape out of reach of the punisher.

I'm sure I needn't belabor any further the notion that warmth is an important variable. But to say this is not enough. We still are faced with considerable difficulty in definition. It has been the experience of a number of people working with child-training data that they find themselves able to make reliable distinctions between mothers they call warm and mothers they call cold, and they find it possible to train others to make similar distinctions, but find it difficult indeed to define exactly what cues they are using to make the rating.

I suspect one source of difficulty is that the behavior we look for as indicating warmth varies with the age of the child the mother is dealing with. When the child is an infant, we are likely to label a mother as warm if she gives a good deal of the contact comfort that Harlow (8) has described. As the child grows older, the part played by the giving of contact comfort in the total constellation of warmth undoubtedly declines. When a child is ten, a mother seldom expresses her warm feelings for him by holding him on her lap. Rather, they are more likely to be expressed by the mother showing interest in the child and what he is doing, by helping unconditionally when help is needed, by being cordial and relaxed. Now warmth as expressed this way is not the same thing as giving contact comfort, and it is not to be expected that the same individuals would necessarily be good at both. Those of you who have read Brody's fascinating, detailed descriptions of mothers' behavior toward their infants (4) will perhaps have noted that the mothers who gave effective contact comfort, in the sense of holding the child comfortably and close, stroking it occasionally, imparting some rocking motion, handling it skillfully and gently in the process of caring for the child—the women who could do all these things well were not necessarily the same women who expressed delight and pride in their children, who noticed their little accomplishments, or who looked upon their infants as individuals. We should therefore not be surprised if there are low correlations between a mother's warmth toward her infant and her warmth toward the same child when it is older. If a primary ingredient of warmth is being able to gratify the child's needs unconditionally, and if the child's needs change from the infantile needs for being fed and being given contact comfort to the more mature needs for various kinds of ego support, then it is necessary for a mother to change considerably as her child changes, in order to be warm towards him at all ages. Some mothers make this change more easily than others. It is true that Schaeffer and Bayley (19), in their longitudinal study of a group of mothers, did find a substantial degree of continuity in the degree of warmth displayed by a given mother toward a given child as the child grew older. There were undoubtedly individual differences in the ways warmth was manifested, and in the appropriateness of a mother's particular style of warmth-giving to the needs of her child at each developmental stage.

From the standpoint of making use of the variable in research, it appears that we should recognize that measuring the mother's current warmth at the time the child is, say, in nursery school or in the primary grades may not be an especially good index of how warm she was to the child as an infant. Further-

more, her warmth in infancy might predict quite different characteristics of the child than her warmth in middle childhood. If there
is any relation at all between nurturance to an infant and its later
personality traits, infant nurturance ought to relate only to those
aspects of personality that presumably have their foundation in
infancy—such as Erikson's dimension of trust (6), or various
aspects of orality. Achievement motivation, on the other hand, if
it is related to the mother's warmth at all, ought to be related to
measures of this variable taken when the child is older. A finding
of Bronfenbrenner's (5) seems to support this point about the
importance of warmth-giving being appropriate to the developmental level of the child. He was studying high-school age
children and employed several variables relating to the kind and
amount of affectionate interchange between these adolescents
and their parents. He measured the parents' affection-giving (in
the sense of direct demonstrativeness), use of affective rewards,
nurturance, and affiliative companionship. Among these variables, it was only the last one, affiliative companionship, that
correlated with the child's current level of responsibility taking.
We can speculate that this particular aspect of warmth is the one
that fits in much better with an adolescent's needs than either
giving him kisses or peanut butter sandwiches. All this means that
warmth has to be defined in terms of parental responsiveness to
the changing needs of the child.

I have referred to socialization variables that came originally
from laboratory studies of learning, and that have been adapted
for use in studying the socialization process. I have also referred
to variables that originated in psychodynamic thinking. There is a
set of variables that is difficult to classify in terms of these two
theoretical systems; I am referring to the dimension "permissiveness vs. restrictiveness," which emerged in our factor analysis of
the *Patterns* variables, and to the related dimension of "control
vs. laissez-faire" which has come out of the factor analysis of the
PARI scales. The theoretical status of these variables is confusing because they relate to both psychoanalytic and learning
theory, but the predictions from the two theories as to the
probable effects of "permissiveness" or "control" are sometimes
quite different. To cite a familiar example, there is the issue of
what ought to be the effects of permissive treatment of the

infant's sucking responses. The question is complex, but a simplified version of the opposing positions would be this: the learning theorist would argue that if an infant is permitted extensive sucking, his sucking habit will be strengthened, and he will be more likely to suck his thumb, pencils, etc., at a later age. The psychodynamic theorist would argue that permitting extensive infantile sucking satisfies oral needs and reduces the likelihood of excessive oral behavior at a later age. The same kind of difference of opinion can be found concerning whether permissive treatment of a child's aggressive or dependent responses should increase or decrease those responses. Now, of course, the fact that different theories produce different predictions concerning the effects of a variable is no reason for abandoning the variable. On the contrary, it is cause for rejoicing, and we should by all means continue to use the variable so that we can get data which will bear upon the validity of the theories. The trouble is that when we arrive at the point of trying to get agreement on the interpretation of findings, it sometimes turns out that the two schools of thought did not mean the same thing by "permissiveness." If a study shows that the more permissive parents are toward their children's aggression the more aggressive the children become, the psychodynamic theorist may say, "Well, by permissiveness I didn't mean *license;* the child must have limits set for him but he must also be allowed to express his feelings." If, on the other hand, a study shows that children heavily punished for aggression are more aggressive on the playground, or prefer aggressive TV programs, the learning theorist may say, "Well, of course, if the parents' methods of stopping aggression are such as to provide additional instigation to aggression, then their non-permissiveness won't eliminate the behavior." We begin to see that there are some hidden meanings in such a term as "permissiveness" and that we are dealing with several dimensions. Continuing with the example of aggression, we can see that permissiveness for aggression could mean the following things:

1. The mother holds the attitude that aggression is an acceptable, even desirable, form of behavior.

2. The mother does not like aggressive behavior and expects to limit it in her children, but feels that it is natural and inevitable

at certain ages and so does not react strongly when her young child displays anger. A related definition of permissiveness would be pacing the demands for self-control placed upon the child to correspond with his developmental level.

3. The mother is not especially interested in the child or is otherwise occupied, and does not act to stop or prevent his aggression because she does not notice what he is doing.

4. The mother does not act early in a sequence of her child's aggressive behavior, but waits till the behavior has become fairly intense.

And at the other end of the scale, the effect of *non*-permissiveness ought to depend upon how the non-permitting is done—whether by punishment, by reinforcing alternative behavior, by environmental control that removes the instigations to undesired behavior, or some other means. The basic point I wish to emphasize is that I believe "permissiveness" is not a unitary variable, and that we need to work more directly with its components.

So far I have discussed several classes of variables: the ones translated as directly as possible from laboratory studies of learning (e.g., amount and kind of reward and punishment), and variables such as warmth and permissiveness of the socializing agent, which have their origins more in psychodynamic theories. There is another class of variables which has been emerging as more and more important, namely the "social structure" variables. These variables have their origin largely in sociological thinking. I do not have time to give them more than the most cursory attention, but I do not believe they can be omitted if we are to do any sort of justice to the scope of significant variables employed in current socialization studies. One has only to list a few findings which have come out of the investigation of social structure factors to see how essential it has become to take them into account. Here is a brief sampling of such findings:

1. With adolescents, parents are most strict with children who are of the same sex as the dominant parent (17).

2. A mother's use of strongly dominant child-rearing tech-

niques (called "unqualified power assertion" in this study) is related to her husband's F score (authoritarian personality score), but not to her own (11).

3. A mother's behavior toward her children is more closely related to her husband's education than her own, and her behavior is more closely related to her husband's education than is *his* behavior to his own education. Thus it appears that it is the family's social status, as indicated by the husband's education, that influences the mother's socialization practices (5).

4. Sons are more intra-punitive if their mothers are primarily responsible for discipline than they are if their fathers are the primary disciplinarians (10).

5. Aspects of social organization such as whether residence is patrilocal, matrilocal, or neolocal, and whether marriage is polygamous or monogamous, determine such aspects of culture as the length of the postpartum sex taboo, the duration of exclusive mother-child sleeping arrangements, and the amount of authority the father has over the child; these factors in turn influence such socialization practices as the age of weaning, the severity of the socialization pressures which are directed toward breaking up the child's dependency upon the mother, and the existence and nature of puberty rites at adolescence. These socialization practices then in their turn influence certain aspects of personality, including certain culturally established defense systems (24, 25, 26).

6. When offered a choice between a small piece of candy now vs. a large one later, children from father-present homes can postpone gratification more easily than children from father-absent homes (15).

These findings all represent efforts to put socialization practices into a cultural or social-structural context. In each case, socialization practices are regarded as a link in a several-step chain, and consideration is given to the factors which determine the socialization practices themselves, as well as to the effects these practices in their turn have upon the child. It is clear that the way parents treat their children will be a function of their relationship to each other (especially of the distribution of authority between them), of the place the family has in the status system of the society in which the family resides, of the society's kinship system, etc. Of course, not every student of socialization need concern himself with all the steps in the complex sequence; he may, and often does, select a set of socialization practices and relate them to the child's behavior without going back to the conditions which led to these practices. But he needs to be aware of the degree to which socialization practices are embedded in a cultural context, and even needs to be alert to the possibility that the "same" socialization practice may have different effects when it is part of different cultural settings. So far, few studies have been planned or analyzed with this possibility in mind, but it might be worth some empirical examination.

It is time to make explicit an assumption that has been implicit so far about the constancy of personality from one situation to another and from one time to another. When we select aspects of parental behavior to study, and try to relate these to measured characteristics of the child, we usually measure what we believe to be reasonably pervasive, reasonably enduring "traits" of the parent and child. Orville Brim (3) in a recent paper, has leveled a direct attack at the notion of trait constancy. He has asserted that there is no such thing as a "warm" person, nor an "aggressive" person, nor a "dependent" person, but that behavior is specific to roles. This would mean that the same individual may be aggressive with his subordinates and dependent toward his boss; that a child may be emotionally expressive with his same-sexed age mates, but not with his teachers or his parents. The question of exactly how general personality traits are, is, of course, a matter that personality theorists have struggled with for many years. But our view of this matter will have some bearing upon our selection and definition of socialization variables. For if a child's behavior is going to be entirely specific to roles, then there is no point in trying to predict any generalized traits in the child; rather, we should be looking for those aspects of the socialization situation that will determine what behavior will be adopted by the child in each different role relationship in which he will find himself. If we wanted to find what socialization practices were associated with the child's becoming dominant or submissive, for example, we would have to study how his dominant behavior had been reacted to when he was playing with same-sexed siblings, and study this separately from the socialization of the same behavior when he was playing with opposite-sexed siblings. Only thus could we predict, according to Brim, how dominant he would be with other boys in the classroom; and we would have to make a separate prediction of his dominance with girls in the classroom. We have already been following Brim's advice, in essence, when we do studies in which we test how the child's behavior varies with the role characteristics of the person with whom he is interacting. A good example is Gewirtz' and Baer's study on the interaction between the sex of the experimenter and the effects of interrupted nurturance (7). But to follow Brim's point further, we would have to investigate the ways in which the child's behavior toward specific categories of "others" was conditioned by differential socialization in these role relationships.

I do not believe that either socialization or the child's reaction tendencies are as role-specific as Brim claims; but obviously role differentiation does occur, and he is quite right in calling our attention to the fact that, for some variables at least, we should be studying socialization separately within roles. Actually, role is only one aspect of situational variability; we have known ever since the days of Hartshorne and May (9) that trait behavior like "honesty" is situation-specific. They found, for example, that the child who will cheat on the playground is not necessarily the same child who will cheat in the classroom, and that cheating is a function of the specific task presented to the child. This means that, in studying the effects of socialization, we either have to abandon efforts to predict characteristics like "honesty" and attempt to study only those characteristics of the child that are at least somewhat constant across situations, or we have to choose socialization variables that are themselves much more situation-specific, and make much more detailed predictions. An example of the utility of making socialization variables more specific to the situations they are intended to predict is provided in a study by Levy (13), in which it was found that a child's adjustment to a hospital experience was *not* a function of the parents having trained the child generally to meet many different kinds of stress situations; rather, the child's response to hospitalization was predicted only from the amount of training the parent gave in advance for the meeting of this *particular* stress situation.

The same sort of situation prevails with respect to trait constancy over time. In their recent article on dependency, Kagan and Moss (12) were able to present repeated measurements of dependency in the same group of individuals—measurements which began at the age of three and continued into the late twenties. The most notable feature of their findings was the absence of continuity in this trait. The children who were dependent at age three and four were not the same individuals who emerged as dependent in adulthood. There was simply no continuity at all for boys, while there was some, but not a great deal, for girls. Let us consider Kagan's findings from the standpoint of efforts to study the socialization practices that are related to dependency. The first and obvious point is that we cannot expect to find any characteristic of the parent's behavior that will correlate with dependency in the young child and also correlate with dependency when the child is an adolescent or adult. This is not to say that the only correlations we can hope for are those between socialization practices and child characteristics measured at the same point in time. It is of course most likely that we shall be able to find aspects of a parent's current behavior that correlate with characteristics his child is displaying at the same time. But it is also possible that we could find aspects of the parent's current behavior whose effects will not show up until later. That is, perhaps there were things the parents of Kagan's sample of children were doing when these children were three and four that had some bearing upon how dependent the children became at the age of ten or eleven. But it is clear enough that whatever these delayed-action variables are, they could hardly be the same variables as the ones which determined how dependent the children were at age three, since it was not the same children who were displaying large amounts of dependency behavior at the two ages.

I have pointed to the way in which different theoretical systems, and different social-science disciplines, have converged to define and elaborate some of the variables which have been used in studies of socialization. In some cases this convergence has produced useful new knowledge; in others it has produced confusion over the meaning of variables. More importantly, it has produced a startling range of findings which have not yet been integrated into a theory of socialization. This is a major task that remains to be done.

REFERENCES

1. Allinsmith, B. 1960. Directness with which anger is expressed. In D. R. Miller and G. E. Swanson (eds.), *Inner conflict and defense*. New York: Holt-Dryden.
2. Baldwin, A. L.; J. Kalhorn; and F. H. Breese. 1949. The appraisal of parent behavior. *Psychological Monographs* 63, no. 4.
3. Brim, O. G. 1960. Personality development as role learning. In I. Iscoe and H. Stevenson (eds.), *Personality development in children*. Austin: University of Texas Press.
4. Brody, S. 1957. *Patterns of mothering*. New York: International Universities Press.
5. Bronfenbrenner, U. 1959. Some familial antecedents of responsibility and leadership in adolescents. Dittoed paper. Ithaca, N.Y.: Cornell University.
6. Erikson, E. H. 1950. *Childhood and society*. New York: Norton.
7. Gewirtz, J. L., and D. M. Baer. 1956. Does brief social "deprivation" enhance the effectiveness of a social reinforcer ("approval")? *American Psychologist* 11: 428–29.
8. Harlow, H. F. 1958. On the nature of love. *American Psychologist* 13: 673–85.
9. Hartshorne, H., and M. A. May. 1928. *Studies in deceit*. New York: Macmillan.
10. Henry, A. F. 1956. Family role structure and self-blame. *Social Forces* 35: 34–38.
11. Hoffman, M. L. 1960. Power assertion by parents and its impact on the child. *Child Development* 31: 129–44.
12. Kagan, J., and H. A. Moss. 1960. The stability of passive and dependent behavior from childhood through adulthood. *Child Development* 31: 577–91.
13. Levy, E. 1959. Children's behavior under stress and its relation to training by parents to respond to stress situation. *Child Development* 30: 307–24.
14. McCord, W., and J. McCord. 1959. *The origins of crime*. New York: Columbia University Press.
15. Mischel, W. 1958. Preference for delayed reinforcement: An experimental study of cultural observation. *Journal of Abnormal and Social Psychology* 56: 57–61.
16. Munn, N. L. 1955. *The evolution and growth of human behavior*. Boston: Houghton Mifflin.
17. Papanek, M. L. 1954. Family structure and child-training practices. Ph.D. dissertation. Cambridge, Mass.: Radcliffe College.
18. Roff, M. 1949. A factorial study of the Fels parent behavior scales. *Child Development* 20: 29–45.

19. Schaeffer, E. S., and N. Bayley. 1960. Consistency of maternal behavior from infancy to pre-adolescence. *Journal of Abnormal and Social Psychology* 61: 1–6.
20. Schaeffer, E. S., and R. Q. Bell. 1958. Development of a parental attitude research instrument. *Child Development* 29: 339–61.
21. Sears, R. R.; Eleanor E. Maccoby; and H. Levin. 1957. *Patterns of child rearing.* Evanston, Ill.: Row, Peterson.
22. Shoben, E. J. 1949. The assessment of parental attitudes in relation to child adjustment. *Genetic Psychology Monographs* 39.
23. Watson, R. I. 1959. *Psychology of the child.* New York: Wiley.
24. Whiting, J. W. M. 1959. Sin, sorcery and the superego. In M. R. Jones (ed.), *Nebraska symposium on motivation.* Lincoln: University of Nebraska Press.
25. Whiting, J. W. M.; E. H. Chasdi; H. F. Antonovsky; and B. C. Ayres. (In press at time of writing.) The learning of values. In F. Kluckhohn and E. Vogt (eds.), *The peoples of Rimrock: A comparative study of values systems.*
26. Whiting, J. W. M.; R. Kluckhohn; and A. Anthony. 1958. The functions of male initiation rites at puberty. In Eleanor E. Maccoby; T. M. Newcomb; and E. L. Hartley (eds.), *Readings in social psychology.* New York: Holt.
27. Zuckerman, M.; B. Barrett-Ribback; I. Monashkin; and J. Norton. 1958. Normative data and factor analysis on the parental attitude research instrument. *Journal of Consulting Psychology* 22: 165–71.

3

The Process of Learning Parental and Sex-Role Identification

DAVID B. LYNN

The purpose of this paper is to summarize the writer's theoretical formulation concerning identification, much of which has been published piecemeal in various journals. Research relevant to new hypotheses is cited, and references are given to previous publications of this writer in which the reader can find evidence concerning the earlier hypotheses. Some of the previously published hypotheses are considerably revised in this paper and, it is hoped, placed in a more comprehensive and coherent framework.

THEORETICAL FORMULATION

Before developing specific hypotheses, one must briefly define identification as it is used here. _Parental identification refers to the internalization of personality characteristics of one's own parent and to unconscious reactions similar to that parent._

David B. Lynn, "The Process of Learning Parental and Sex-Role Identification," _Journal of Marriage and the Family_ 28, no. 4 (November 1966): 466–70.

Presented at the Annual Meeting of the American Orthopsychiatric Association, 1966.

This is to be contrasted with *sex-role identification,* which refers to the internalization of the role typical of a given sex in a particular culture and to the unconscious reactions characteristic of that role. Thus, theoretically, an individual might be thoroughly identified with the role typical of his own sex generally and yet poorly identified with his same-sex parent specifically. This differentiation also allows for the converse circumstances wherein a person is well identified with his same-sex parent specifically and yet poorly identified with the typical same-sex role generally. In such an instance the parent with whom the individual is well identified is himself poorly identified with the typical sex role. An example might be a girl who is closely identified with her mother, who herself is more strongly identified with the masculine than with the feminine role. Therefore, such a girl, through her identification with her mother, is poorly identified with the feminine role.[1]

Formulation of Hypotheses

It is postulated that the initial parental identification of both male and female infants is with the mother. Boys, but not girls, must shift from this initial mother identification and establish masculine-role identification. Typically in this culture the girl has the same-sex parental model for identification (the mother) with her more hours per day than the boy has his same-sex model (the father) with him. Moreover, even when home, the father does not usually participate in as many intimate activities with the child as does the mother, e.g., preparation for bed, toileting. The time spent with the child and the intimacy and intensity of the contact are thought to be pertinent to the process of learning parental identification.[2] The boy is seldom if ever with the father as he engages in his daily vocational activities, although both boy and girl are often with the mother as she goes through her household activities. Consequently, the father, as a model for the boy, is

[1] D. B. Lynn, *"Sex-Role and Parental Identification," Child Development* 33, no. 3 (1962): 555–64.

[2] B. A. Goodfield, "A Preliminary Paper on the Development of the Time Intensity Compensation Hypothesis in Masculine Identification," paper read at the San Francisco State Psychological Convention (April 1965).

analogous to a map showing the major outline but lacking most details, whereas the mother, as a model for the girl, might be thought of as a detailed map.

However, despite the shortage of male models, a somewhat stereotyped and conventional masculine role is nonetheless spelled out for the boy, often by his mother and women teachers in the absence of his father and male models. Through the reinforcement of the culture's highly developed system of rewards for typical masculine-role behavior and punishment for signs of femininity, the boy's early learned identification with the mother weakens. Upon this weakened mother identification is welded the later learned identification with a culturally defined, stereotyped masculine role.

(1) Consequently, males tend to identify with a culturally defined masculine role, whereas females tend to identify with their mothers.[3] (Specific hypothesis are numbered and in italics.)

Although one must recognize the contribution of the father in the identification of males and the general cultural influences in the identification of females, it nevertheless seems meaningful, for simplicity in developing this formulation, to refer frequently to *masculine-role identification* in males as distinguished from *mother identification* in females.

Some evidence is accumulating suggesting that (2) *both males and females identify more closely with the mother than with the father.* Evidence is found in support of this hypothesis in a study by Lazowick[4] in which the subjects were 30 college students. These subjects and their mothers and fathers were required to rate concepts, e.g., "myself," "father," "mother," etc. The degree of semantic similarity as rated by the subjects and their parents was determined. The degree of similarity between fathers and their own children was not significantly greater than that found between fathers and children randomly matched. However, children did share a greater semantic similarity with their own mothers than they did when matched at random with

---

[3]D. B. Lynn, "A Note on Sex Differences in the Development of Masculine and Feminine Identification," *Psychological Review* 66, no. 2 (1959): 126–35.

[4]L. M. Lazowick, "On the Nature of Identification," *Journal of Abnormal and Social Psychology* 51 (1955): 175–83.

other maternal figures. Mothers and daughters did not share a significantly greater semantic similarity than did mothers and sons.

Evidence is also found in support of Hypothesis 2 in a study by Adams and Sarason[5] using anxiety scales with male and female high-school students and their mothers and fathers. They found that anxiety scores of both boys and girls were much more related to mothers' than to fathers' anxiety scores.

Support for this hypothesis comes from a study in which Aldous and Kell[6] interviewed 50 middle-class college students and their mothers concerning childrearing values. They found, contrary to their expectation, that a slightly higher proportion of boys than girls shared their mothers' childrearing values.

Partial support for Hypothesis 2 is provided in a study by Gray and Klaus[7] using the Allport-Vernon-Lindzey Study of Values completed by 34 female and 28 male college students and by their parents. They found that the men were not significantly closer to their fathers than to their mothers and also that the men were not significantly closer to their fathers than were the women. However, the women were closer to their mothers than were the men and closer to their mothers than to their fathers.

Note that, in reporting research relevant to Hypothesis 2, only studies of *tested similarity,* not *perceived similarity,* were reviewed. To test this hypothesis, one must measure tested similarity, i.e., measure both the child and the parent on the same variable and compare the similarity between these two measures. This paper is not concerned with perceived similarity, i.e., testing the child on a given variable and then comparing that finding with a measure taken as to how the child thinks his parent would respond. It is this writer's opinion that much confusion has arisen by considering perceived similarity as a measure of parental identification. It seems obvious that, especially for the male, perceived similarity between father and son would usually be closer than tested similarity, in that it is socially desirable for a

[5] E. B. Adams and I. G. Sarason, "Relation Between Anxiety in Children and Their Parents," *Child Development* 34, no. 1 (1963): 237–46.

[6] J. Aldous and L. Kell, "A Partial Test of Some Theories of Identification," *Marriage and Family Living* 23, no. 1 (1961): 15–19.

[7] S. W. Gray and R. Klaus, "The Assessment of Parental Identification," *Genetic Psychology Monographs* 54 (1956): 87–114.

man to be similar to his father, especially as contrasted to his similarity to his mother. Indeed, Gray and Klaus[8] found the males' perceived similarity with the father to be closer than tested similarity.

It is hypothesized that the closer identification of males with the mother than with the father will be revealed more clearly on some measures than on others. (3) *The closer identification of males with their mothers than with their fathers will be revealed most frequently in personality variables which are not clearly sex-typed.* In other words, males are more likely to be more similar to their mothers than to their fathers in variables in which masculine and feminine role behavior is not especially relevant in the culture.

There has been too little research on tested similarity between males and their parents to presume an adequate test of Hypothesis 3. In order to test it, one would first have to judge personality variables as to how typically masculine or feminine they seem. One could then test to determine whether a higher proportion of males are more similar to their mothers than to their fathers on those variables which are not clearly sex-typed, rather than on those which are judged clearly to be either masculine or feminine. To this writer's knowledge, this has not been done.

It is postulated that the task of achieving these separate kinds of identification (masculine role for males and mother identification for females) requires separate methods of learning for each sex. These separate methods of learning to identify seem to be problem-solving for boys and lesson-learning for girls. Woodworth and Schlosberg differentiate between the task of solving problems and that of learning lessons in the following way:

> With a problem to master the learner must explore the situation and find the goal before his task is fully presented. In the case of a lesson, the problem-solving phase is omitted or at least minimized, as we see when the human subject is instructed to memorize this poem or that list of nonsense syllables, to examine these pictures with a view to recognizing them later.[9]

[8]Gray and Klaus, "The Assessment of Parental Identification."
[9]R. S. Woodworth and H. Schlosberg, *Experimental Psychology* (New York: Holt, 1954), p. 529.

Since the girl is not required to shift from the mother in learning her identification, she is expected mainly to learn the mother-identification lesson as it is presented to her, partly through imitation and through the mother's selective reinforcement of mother-similar behavior. She need not abstract principles defining the feminine role to the extent that the boy must in defining the masculine role. Any bit of behavior on the mother's part may be modeled by the girl in learning the mother-identification lesson.

However, finding the appropriate identification goal does constitute a major problem for the boy in solving the masculine-role identification problem. When the boy discovers that he does not belong in the same sex category as the mother, he must then find the proper sex-role identification goal. Masculine-role behavior is defined for him through admonishments, often negatively given, e.g., the mother's and teachers' telling him that he should not be a sissy without precisely indicating what he *should* be. Moreover, these negative admonishments are made in the early grades in the absence of male teachers to serve as models and with the father himself often unavailable as a model. The boy must restructure these admonishments in order to abstract principles defining the masculine role. It is this process of defining the masculine-role goal which is involved in solving the masculine-role identification problem.

One of the basic steps in this formulation can now be taken. (4) *In learning the sex-typical identification, each sex is thereby acquiring separate methods of learning which are subsequently applied to learning tasks generally.*[10]

The little girl acquires a learning method which primarily involves (a) a personal relationship, and (b) imitation rather than restructuring the field and abstracting principles. On the other hand, the little boy acquires a different learning method which primarily involves (a) defining the goal, (b) restructuring the field, and (c) abstracting principles. There are a number of findings which are consistent with Hypothesis 4, such as the frequently reported greater problem-solving skill of males and the greater field dependence of females.[11]

[10]Lynn, "Sex-Role and Parental Identification."
[11]Lynn, "Sex-Role and Parental Identification."

The shift of the little boy from mother identification to masculine-role identification is assumed to be frequently a crisis. It has been observed that demands for typical sex-role behavior come at an earlier age for boys than for girls. These demands are made at an age when boys are least able to understand thèm. As was pointed out above, demands for masculine sex-role behavior are often made by women in the absence of readily available male models to demonstrate typical sex-role behavior. Such demands are often presented in the form of punishing, *negative* admonishments, i.e., telling the boy what not to do rather than what to do and backing up the demands with punishment. These are thought to be very different conditions from those in which the girl learns her mother-identification lesson. Such methods of demanding typical sex-role behavior of boys are very poor methods for inducing learning.

(5) *Therefore, males tend to have greater difficulty in achieving same-sex identification than females.*[12]

(6) *Furthermore, more males than females fail more or less completely in achieving same-sex identification, but they rather make an opposite-sex identification.*[13]

Negative admonishments given at an age when the child is least able to understand them and supported by punishment are thought to produce anxiety concerning sex-role behavior. In Hartley's words:

> This situation gives us practically a perfect combination for inducing anxiety—the demand that the child do something which is not clearly defined to him, based on reasons he cannot possibly appreciate, and enforced with threats, punishments and anger by those who are close to him.[14]

(7) *Consequently, males are more anxious regarding sex-role*

[12]D. B. Lynn, "Divergent Feedback and Sex-Role Identification in Boys and Men," *Merrill-Palmer Quarterly* 10, no. 1 (1964): 17–23.
[13]D. B. Lynn, "Sex Differences in Identification Development," *Sociometry* 24, no. 4 (1961): 372–83.
[14]R. E. Hartley, "Sex-Role Pressures and the Socialization of the Male Child," *Psychological Reports* 5 (1959): 458.

identification than females.[15] It is postulated that punishment often leads to dislike of the activity that led to punishment.[16] Since it is "girl-like" activities that provoked the punishment administered in an effort to induce sex-typical behavior in boys, then, in developing dislike for the activity which led to such punishment, boys should develop hostility toward "girl-like" activities. Also, boys should be expected to generalize and consequently develop hostility toward all females as representatives of this disliked role. There is not thought to be as much pressure on girls as on boys to avoid opposite-sex activities. It is assumed that girls are punished neither so early nor so severely for adopting masculine sex-role behavior.

(8) *Therefore, males tend to hold stronger feelings of hostility toward females than females toward males.*[17] The young boy's same-sex identification is at first not very firm because of the shift from mother to masculine identification. On the other hand, the young girl, because she need make no shift in identification, remains relatively firm in her mother identification. However, the culture, which is male-dominant in orientation, reinforces the boy's developing masculine-role identification much more thoroughly than it does the girl's developing feminine identification. He is rewarded simply for having been born masculine through countless privileges accorded males but not females. As Brown pointed out:

> The superior position and privileged status of the male permeates nearly every aspect, minor and major, of our social life. The gadgets and prizes in boxes of breakfast cereal, for example, commonly have a strong masculine rather than feminine appeal. And the most basic social institutions perpetuate this pattern of masculine aggrandizement. Thus, the Judeo-Christian faiths involve worshipping God, a "Father," rather

[15]Lynn, "Divergent Feedback and Sex-Role Identification in Boys and Men."

[16]E. R. Hilgard, *Introduction to Psychology* (New York: Harcourt, Brace, and World, 1962).

[17]Lynn, "Divergent Feedback and Sex-Role Identification in Boys and Men."

than a "Mother," and Christ, a "Son," rather than a "Daughter."[18]

(9) *Consequently, with increasing age, males become relatively more firmly identified with the masculine role.*[19]

Since psychological disturbances should, theoretically, be associated with inadequate same-sex identification and since males are postulated to be gaining in masculine identification, the following is predicted: (10) *With increasing age males develop psychological disturbances at a more slowly accelerating rate than females.*[20]

It is postulated that as girls grow older, they become increasingly disenchanted with the feminine role because of the prejudices against their sex and the privileges and prestige offered the male rather than the female. Even the women with whom they come in contact are likely to share the prejudices prevailing in this culture against their own sex.[21] Smith[22] found that with increasing age girls have a progressively better opinion of boys and a progressively poorer opinion of themselves. (11) *Consequently, a larger proportion of females than males show preference for the role of the opposite sex.*[23]

Note that in Hypothesis 11 the term "preference" rather than "identification" was used. It is *not* hypothesized that a larger proportion of females than males *identify* with the opposite sex (Hypothesis 6 predicted the reverse) but rather that they will show *preference* for the role of the opposite sex. *Sex-role preference* refers to the desire to adopt the behavior associated with one sex or the other or the perception of such behavior as preferable or more desirable. *Sex-role preference* should be contrasted with *sex-role identification,* which, as stated previously, refers to the

[18]D. G. Brown, "Sex-Role Development in a Changing Culture," *Psychological Bulletin* 55 (1958): 235.

[19]Lynn, "A Note on Sex Differences in the Development of Masculine and Feminine Identification."

[20]Lynn, "Sex Differences in Identification Development."

[21]P. M. Kitay, "A Comparison of the Sexes in Their Attitudes and Beliefs About Women: A Study of Prestige Groups," *Sociometry* 3 (1940): 399–407.

[22]S. Smith, "Age and Sex Differences in Children's Opinion Concerning Sex Differences," *Journal of Genetic Psychology* 54 (1939): 17–25.

[23]Lynn, "A Note on Sex Differences in the Development of Masculine and Feminine Identification."

actual incorporation of the role of a given sex and to the unconscious reactions characteristic of that role.

Punishment may suppress behavior without causing its un-learning.[24] Because of the postulated punishment administered to males for adopting opposite-sex role behavior, it is predicted that males will repress atypical sex-role behavior rather than unlearn it. One might predict, then, a discrepancy between the underlying sex-role identification and the overt sex-role behavior of males. For females, on the other hand, no comparable punishment for adopting many aspects of the opposite-sex role is postulated. (12) *Consequently, where a discrepancy exists between sex-role prefer-ence and identification, it will tend to be as follows: Males will tend to show same-sex role preference with underlying opposite-sex identification. Females will tend to show opposite-sex role preference with underlying same-sex identification.*[25] Stated in another way, where a discrepancy occurs both males and females will tend to show masculine-role preference with underlying feminine identification.

Not only is the masculine role accorded more prestige than the feminine role, but males are more likely than females to be ridiculed or punished for adopting aspects of the opposite-sex role. For a girl to be a tomboy does not involve the censure that results when a boy is a sissy. Girls may wear masculine clothing (shirts and trousers), but boys may not wear feminine clothing (skirts and dresses). Girls may play with toys typically associated with boys (cars, trucks, erector sets, and guns), but boys are discouraged from playing with feminine toys (dolls and tea sets). (13) *Therefore, a higher proportion of females than males adopt aspects of the role of the opposite sex.*[26]

Note that Hypothesis 13 refers to *sex-role adoption* rather than *sex-role identification* or *preference*. *Sex-role adoption* refers to the overt behavior characteristic of a given sex. An example contrasting sex-role adoption with preference and identification is an individual who *adopts* behavior characteristic of his own sex

[24]Hilgard, *Introduction to Psychology.*

[25]Lynn, "Divergent Feedback and Sex-Role Identification in Boys and Men."

[26]Lynn, "A Note on Sex Differences in the Development of Masculine and Feminine Identification."

because it is expedient, not because he *prefers* it nor because he is so *identified*.

Summary

The purpose of this paper has been to summarize the writer's theoretical formulation and to place it in a more comprehensive and coherent framework. The following hypotheses were presented and discussed:

1. Males tend to identify with a culturally defined masculine role, whereas females tend to identify with their mothers.

2. Both males and females identify more closely with the mother than with the father.

3. The closer identification of males with their mothers than with their fathers will be revealed most frequently in personality variables which are not clearly sex-typed.

4. In learning the sex-typical identification, each sex is thereby acquiring separate methods of learning which are subsequently applied to learning tasks generally.

5. Males tend to have greater difficulty in achieving same-sex identification than females.

6. More males than females fail more or less completely in achieving same-sex identification but rather make an opposite-sex identification.

7. Males are more anxious regarding sex-role identification than females.

8. Males tend to hold stronger feelings of hostility toward females than females toward males.

9. With increasing age, males become relatively more firmly identified with the masculine role.

10. With increasing age, males develop psychological disturbances at a more slowly accelerating rate than females.

11. A larger proportion of females than males show preference for the role of the opposite sex.

12. Where a discrepancy exists between sex-role preference and identification, it will tend to be as follows: Males will tend to show same-sex role preference with underlying opposite-sex

identification. Females will tend to show opposite-sex role preference with underlying same-sex identification.

13. A higher proportion of females than males adopt aspects of the role of the opposite sex.

4

Some New Perspectives
on Upward Mobility

ROBERT A. ELLIS

The stratification literature reveals that the key to understanding the mobility process lies in part in the internal variables of intelligence and motivation (cf. Perrucci, 1967; Rosen, Crockett, & Nunn, 1969).* The chances of getting the educational advantages which make mobility possible—and then of being able to capitalize on those advantages—increase directly as a function of measured intellectual ability. In addition, the person who is going to improve his status circumstances must apparently experience some dissatisfaction with his present lot in life (or more accurately with his parents' lot in life) and, at the same time, have a need for achievement in which middle-class goals are defined as desirable. It would also appear to be important that the mobile individual gains the view that these goals are feasible—a level of expectation that makes the aspired objectives seem reachable (cf. Keller & Zavalloni, 1964).

Robert A. Ellis, "Some New Perspectives on Upward Mobility," *Urban and Social Change Review* 4, no. 1 (Fall 1970): 15–17.

Paper read at the annual meeting of the American Sociological Association, August, 1970. The research from which this report was derived has been supported by Public Health Grant MH-15735 from the National Institute of Mental Health.

*The reference list is alphabetical by author at the end of the chapter.

Yet, it is also evident that social mobility does not occur in a social vacuum. As the writer has noted in an earlier paper (Ellis & Lane, 1963), "lower-class youth (generally) find themselves confronted by an environment in which going to college is the exception, not the rule, and in which strong counterpressures may be mounted against those who seek to deviate from prevailing cultural norms" (p. 743). Consequently, if middle-class educational goals are to emerge among lower-class youth, some substitute channels must exist for transmitting information about educational arrangements and practices that is as a matter of course handed down by parents to children from more favored class backgrounds. In addition, the negative pressures of the environment require that some intermediate social support be available to sustain the mobile individual when the occasion arises for him to sever ties with peers from his class of origin who do not possess educational aspirations to match his own.

These considerations have led to considerable research on the structural supports that enable lower-class youth to use higher education as a mobility channel. In most of these inquiries, the primary focus has been on locating and specifying the *role categories* (e.g., parents, teachers, and peers) which assume special significance in prompting adolescents from disadvantaged backgrounds to go to college. The findings which have been obtained are somewhat uneven and occasionally contradictory. Nevertheless, there is a sufficiently common pattern to the results to suggest that the following propositions may have a wide range of empirical applicability:

1. *The impetus for mobility has its roots in the nuclear family. It is generally found that the decision by a student from the lower class to go to college is one that is made with the approval and support of one or both parents.* In many cases, parents have transmitted to their offspring their own frustrated motivation to get ahead in the world. In some instances, however, where a downwardly mobile parent is involved, the parental pressures for achievement reflect a desire on the part of the parent to recoup lost status advantages.

2. For reasons that are not yet fully understood, *a readily discernible pattern of maternal influence characterizes the family structure of the upwardly mobile.* There is a distinct and wide-

spread tendency for mothers in this group to be singled out as the more influential parent in stimulating mobility behavior. At the same time, one is apt to find in these families evidence that the mother has attained the educational level or occupational status that is markedly superior to the father's. Thus, while the father's continued presence in the family may contribute a stability that is needed if the children are to realize their mobility ambitions, it also would appear likely that the father serves as a negative role model for the mobile youngster. Conversely, it could be expected that if the son too strongly identified with the father he would want to pattern his life after his father's—including having a job like his father.

3. *Successful implementation of their educational plans requires upwardly mobile students to move away from their families for outside support and guidance.* A distinctive dilemma faced by the upwardly mobile is the inability of their parents to shape and give direction to the aspirations they may have stimulated in their children. Students from the lower class must, therefore, depend heavily upon a wide range of persons outside the family (school teachers, adults in the community, and high school peers) for the social learning which would enable them to be effective participants in middle-class society and for the knowledge and judgmental standards needed to give effective direction to their college plans.

These inquiries into the number and type of role categories that assume significance in upward mobility have been fruitful in forcing mobility analysis to go beyond the effects of internal variables such as intelligence and motivation and take account of external variables found in the social structure. Moreover, by underscoring the special dependence of the mobile individual on persons outside the family for help and guidance, these inquiries have provided some clues for understanding the weakening of family ties that accompanies social mobility (cf. Merton, 1957, pp. 269–75, 293–94, 329–30). Nevertheless, *it has become increasingly apparent that it is time to go beyond the question of WHO is important in bringing about social mobility and take up the question of HOW mobility behavior is mediated. What functions do these persons have to perform for mobility goals to emerge and be effectively implemented?*

It is to the latter issue that the remainder of the present paper is directed. The answers to be set forth are provisional and in need of further test. Indeed, the data are highly impressionistic, being derived in part from depth interviews conducted with several selected lower-class college students regarding their undergraduate experiences and in part from reexamination of impromptu comments students in our studies had made in response to probe questions concerning the persons who influenced their decision to come to college or, once at college, their choice of an undergraduate major.

These data, if they can be called that, suggest that it is useful to start with the assumption that social mobility and social maintenance are related processes. In both cases, *there are certain specifiable functions which have to be carried out by persons with whom an individual has significant social contact if (a) a youth from the lower class is going to be able to leave his class of origin and enter the middle class or (b) a youth born in favored status circumstances is going to be able to maintain his station in life.* These functions can be performed by one person alone, but they need not be. They may be performed by a number of different persons either at the same point of time or at different periods of time. Whichever might be the case, *the person, or persons, involved must be able to serve in each of the four following capacities if social mobility or social maintenance is to be realized:*

1. *The goad. This is the person, or set of persons, who prompts an individual to want to achieve a position in which he will be respected and looked up to.* Usually, as it turns out, this function is carried out by some member of the immediate family, although at the lower status levels it is not inevitably the case. However, as has already been noted, there apparently are pronounced social class differences in the likelihood that the father will be the family member who is the prime carrier of achievement values.

2. *The coach. This is the person, or set of persons, who trains an individual in the social and behavioral skills needed for meeting the demands of the middle-class world and gives him the knowledge needed for effectively shaping and directing his life goals.* Coaching, as Strauss (1959, p. 110) has observed, "is an integral

part of teaching the inexperienced—of any age" and is requisite to preparing the inexperienced for the status passages they will traverse. For children from upper-middle-class homes, who are already familiar with the world of the successful college graduate, their parents can directly and indirectly provide the learning experiences that will prepare them for the academic and social demands of college life. In this respect, they have a distinct advantage over children from lower-class backgrounds who usually are the first generation in their family to go to college. This disadvantage is reduced for many upwardly mobile by their ability to turn to persons outside the family for the social learning needed to overcome the subcultural barriers confronting them. Without this "anticipatory socialization," it would be extremely difficult, if not impossible, for the lower-class student to escape the cultural limitations of his environment. Yet, as we have indicated elsewhere (Ellis & Lane, 1966), "There are . . . a number of reasons for considering anticipatory socialization to be a gradual, tentative process, one that even under the best of circumstances only imperfectly prepares the upwardly mobile college student for the middle-class way of life he will encounter" (p. 281).

3. *The incentor. This is the person, or set of persons, who can give to a youth the sympathetic encouragement needed for continuing his career and educational plans despite whatever obstacles and setbacks he may encounter along the way.* The incentor may be aptly described as "the head patter" who provides the incentives to sustain middle-class ambitions. It is a form of support that is especially critical for the mobility aspirant. The family may well socialize him to be dissatisfied with his father's lot in life, but may be unable to provide the realistic incentives needed to give him the expectation that this can be accomplished by going to college. Without such encouragement from some sector of his world—and the expectations of success that result—the mobility aspirant is likely to lose heart and drop out long before his goal is attained.

4. *The sponsor. This is the person, or set of persons, who can open the door to the partially closed systems* (be it college, fraternity, or graduate school) *which an ambitious youth must enter if he is going to be able to carve out a successful middle-class*

career. While there is a considerable body of literature on the part that sponsorship plays in the professions and in industry (cf. Rose, 1969), its significance for social mobility has generally been neglected. In part, this neglect can be traced to the impact of Turner's conceptualization of mobility in the United States as *contest mobility* rather than *sponsored mobility* (Turner, 1960), even though more recently Turner has been persuaded to reformulate his conception of the upward mobility process so as to take into account the idea of sponsorship (Turner, 1966). This reformulation by Turner is consistent with data from our own studies which indicate that sponsorship does operate to facilitate the attainment of mobility goals for selected youth from the lower class. Yet, at the same time, it is also apparent that these youth do not have the same access to sponsorship as do students coming from the upper and upper-middle classes.

Though this treatment of the four functionaries is overly abbreviated, I hope that it is possible to see that their use in research opens some new ways of viewing the mobility process. First of all, it provides a frame of reference for going beyond the question of how mobility goals develop and becoming concerned, instead, with their implementation. *Our basic premise is that the qualified individual, if he is to secure middle-class status, must have each of these functions met by his social environment. If originally he comes from an upper-middle-class background, he has the built-in advantage that all four of these functions can directly or indirectly be met within the immediate family. The student from the lower class, on the other hand, may be stimulated by his parents (and especially by the mother) to improve his lot in life; but to do so, he has to rely on persons outside the family to perform the other functions.* The extent to which he succeeds in doing so will determine whether the mobility aspirant will be able to translate his strivings into actual accomplishments. For those who are successful, such as Warner and Abegglen's (1955) business leaders, this can be an often repeated pattern as the individual moves away from old groups and personal ties and moves toward groups with new values, new habits of behavior (pp. 80–82).

A second advantage of the present approach is the scientific parsimony gained by treating upward mobility, social maintenance, and downward mobility in terms of the same processual variables.

Finally, the social functionary approach corrects what I think is a mistaken, but widely prevailing, notion that mobility in the United States is an open contest. At the very least, it is necessary to recognize that one of the advantages of being born to elite status is the potential access one has to opportunities for sponsorship. This potential, as Mills (1956) and Baltzell (1966) have pointed out, is institutionalized by the metropolitan clubs and exclusive private secondary schools which are patronized by the established elite. In a fundamental respect, it represents the defining characteristic of what is loosely referred to as "the Establishment."

References

Baltzell, E. D. 1966. *The protestant establishment.* New York: Vintage Books, Random House.

Ellis, R. A., and W. C. Lane. 1963. Structural supports for upward mobility. *American Sociological Review* 28: 743.

Ellis, R. A., and W. C. Lane. 1966. Social mobility and career orientation. *Sociology and Social Research* (April): 281.

Keller, Suzanne, and Marisa Zavalloni. 1964. Ambition and social class: A respecification. *Social Forces* 43: 58–70.

Merton, R. K. 1957. *Social theory and social structure,* rev. ed. Glencoe, Ill.: Free Press.

Mills, C. W. 1956. *The power elite.* New York: Oxford.

Perrucci, R. 1967. Education, stratification, and mobility. In D. A. Hansen and J. Gerstl (eds.), *On education: Sociological perspectives.* New York: Wiley.

Rose, R. L. 1969. Career sponsorship in the school superintendency. Unpublished dissertation. Eugene: University of Oregon.

Rosen, B. C.; H. C. Crockett, Jr.; and C. Z. Nunn. 1969. *Achievement in American society.* Cambridge, Mass.: Schenkman.

Strauss, A. 1959. *Mirrors and masks.* New York: Free Press.

Turner, R. H. 1960. Sponsored and contest mobility and the school system. *American Sociological Review* 25: 855–67.

Turner, R. H. 1966. Acceptance of irregular mobility in Britain and the United States. *Sociometry* (December): 335–38.

Warner, W. L., and J. C. Abegglen. 1955. *Big business leaders in America.* New York: Harper.

B. Identification:
Process and Product

5

Child-Rearing Antecedents of Masculine Identification in Kindergarten Boys

PAUL MUSSEN and LUTHER DISTLER

The concept of identification is undoubtedly one of the most prominent in the literature on personality development. Theoretical discussions of the concept are numerous (e.g., 2, 7, 8, 9, 12, 14, 17), and recently there have been a number of studies testing hypotheses derived from these theoretical writings (e.g., 13, 15, 18, 20).

Paul Mussen and Luther Distler, "Child-Rearing Antecedents of Masculine Identification in Kindergarten Boys," *Child Development* 31, no. 1 (March 1960): 89–100. Copyright © 1960 by The Society for Research in Child Development, Inc. All rights reserved. Footnotes have been renumbered.

The authors wish to thank Mr. A. B. Campbell, Assistant Superintendent of Schools of Berkeley, Mr. C. B. Johnson, Principal of the Jefferson School, and Mrs. C. B. Holmes and Mrs. E. P. Light, kindergarten teachers, for their cooperation in this and the earlier study.

Empirical investigations of the concept have customarily used, as operational indices of degree of identification with parents, measures of either (a) degree of "real" or "assumed" similarity between parent and child (4, 15, 24), or (b) personality characteristics or behavioral manifestations which are presumably consequents of the identification process, e.g., aggression (10), high conscience (20), use of the father doll in play (18).

Hypotheses about the antecedents and consequents of strong or weak identification with parents are tested by correlating an index of identification with measures of theoretically relevant variables. Thus, using the amount of use of the father doll as an index of identification with the father, Pauline Sears (18) showed that five-year-old boys with warm and affectionate fathers (as judged from interviews) identified with them more strongly. Similarly, it has been found that adolescent boys who respond to personality and attitude tests as their fathers do—a consequence of the boys' strong identifications with their fathers—are more likely, according to projective test responses, to view their fathers as highly nurturant and rewarding (15). According to another study, a high degree of conscience development in kindergarten children, presumably an index of parental identification, is related to the mother's warmth and acceptance and to her use of withdrawal of love as a method of control. For boys, acceptance by the father was also found to be related to this index (20).

Adequate sex-typing, or acquisition of the personality characteristics, behavior, and attitudes appropriate to the child's own sex, is generally considered to be a major consequent of strong identification with the like-sexed parent (12, 19). For this reason the present authors, in an earlier study, used a measure of sex-typing of interests in young boys as an index of identification with the father (13). In that study three hypotheses about the antecedents of identification were tested by comparing the responses of two groups of five-year-old boys—one group high and one group low in masculinity as measured by the ITSC (3)—to nine semistructured familial doll play stories. Analyses of the doll play protocols indicated that highly masculine (i.e., highly father identified) boys viewed their fathers as powerful sources of both reward and punishment. These data thus seemed to support both the developmental and defensive hypotheses of identification, i.e., boys highly identified with their fathers perceived them as more nurturant and rewarding (as the developmental identification hypothesis would predict) *and* as more threatening and punitive (in accordance with the defensive identification hypothesis). The authors concluded, however, that "role theory with its explicit emphasis on the importance of both reward and punishment in role learning best integrates all these data" (13, p. 17).

It must be emphasized that these findings on correlates of masculinity were based only on the child's *perceptions* of his relationship with his parents, as these were reflected in his doll play. The present study, essentially an extension of the earlier one, is focused on the relationship between degree of sex-typing in young boys and their parents' child-rearing practices. Information on these practices was obtained from interviews with the mothers.[1]

The purpose of the study was to test three major hypotheses (developmental, defensive, and role-taking) about the factors underlying the identification process—and thus to check the conclusions of earlier studies—with another, perhaps more objective, kind of data on family relations. More specifically, we wanted to evaluate the behavior of the fathers of the strongly father-identified (i.e., highly masculine) group toward their sons. Do they tend to act (a) warmly and affectionately, (b) punitively and threateningly, or (c) as powerful agents of both rewards and punishments?

Since the interview data of the present study are in many respects like those of the Sears et al. (20) study, including information on conscience development, we could also determine whether or not different presumed consequents of the identification process—high degree of sex-typing and conscience development—are related to each other and are associated with the same child-rearing variables.

[1]The authors are grateful to Mrs. Marie Mustache for her invaluable aid in conducting the interviews and making the ratings.

PROCEDURE

The basic data about child-rearing practices were obtained from the mothers of the kindergarten boys who were subjects in the authors' earlier study of masculinity and identification (13). The boys had been selected from among 38 white boys, pupils in two kindergarten classes of a predominantly middle-class public school, who had been given the IT Scale, a projective test of sex-role preference (3). Nine of the interviewees were the mothers of boys with the highest (most masculine) scores on the ITSC, and ten were the mothers of boys with the lowest (least masculine) scores. It must be emphasized that *all* the data, including those pertaining to fathers' attitudes and practices, are derived from mothers' reports.

For many reasons the interviews had to be limited to between one half hour and one hour; hence the interview schedule was a relatively short one. It consisted of 32 open-ended questions, some of them with suggested probes taken from the interview schedule used by Sears et al. (20, Appendix A). Almost all the questions concerned the areas most directly relevant to theories of identification and to conscience development. They related to restrictions and demands on the child, use of praise in discipline, warmth, affection, and punitiveness of each parent, the child's dependence and his proneness to confess wrongdoing. The following two questions are illustrative:

> How often do you spank X? [Probes: (a) How about your husband? How often does he spank him? (b) For instance, how often has X been spanked in the last two weeks?]
> Now we'd like to talk awhile about X and his father. Will you tell me something about the way they act toward each other? [Probes: (a) For instance, when your husband comes home from work, when X is there, what happens? (b) How about after dinner? (c) What other kinds of things do they do together?]

All the interviews were conducted by a trained social worker who asked the questions in the prescribed order and used the exact wording given in the schedule. She took extensive notes on each interview, recording as much as possible verbatim.

After she had completed all the interviews, the social worker rated each of them on 28 dimensions. The rating scales, taken from Appendix B of *Patterns of Child Rearing* (20), are listed in Table 1.

In order to eliminate any bias in her work, the social worker was not informed of the real purpose of the research until after she had finished all of her work. Therefore, neither her interviews nor her ratings could have been influenced by knowledge of the hypotheses or the method of selecting the interviewees.

RESULTS

Testing the hypotheses required determining the relationships between masculinity status, on the one hand, and child-rearing practices, the child's relationship with his parents, and conscience development, on the other. This was accomplished by comparing the low and high masculinity groups on each of the 28 variables on which they had been rated.

Since the number of subjects in each group was small and the distributions of ratings were not normal, U tests (11) were used to compare rank transformation scores on all ratings of subjects in the two groups. The results of these tests and the significance levels, together with the meanings of the significant differences and trends in the data, are summarized in Table 1.

The two groups differed significantly or almost significantly in seven of the 28 rated variables. There were some additional trends in the data; that is, there were five variables on which the two groups tended to be rated differently, although the differences were not statistically significant. In general, these trends are consistent with, and support, the statistically significant differences between the two groups.

The findings are particularly relevant to three broad areas—father-son relationships, family climate, and conscience development—and will therefore be presented in three sections.

TABLE 1

DIFFERENCES BETWEEN HIGH AND LOW MASCULINITY GROUPS ON RATING
SCALES OF FAMILIAL VARIABLES AND CONSCIENCE DEVELOPMENT

Rating scale	U	p	Direction of differences between groups
Father-son relationships variables			
Father's standard of obedience	35.0	*ns*	
Frequency with which *father* spanks	37.5	*ns*	
How child and father act toward each other	12.0	.001–.01	Highs have more affectionate relations
Amount of caretaking father does now	31.5	.14*	Highs=more caretaking by father
Affectional bond, father to child	13.5	.001–.01	Highs=fathers warmer
Strictness of father	40.5	*ns*	
Mother-son relationships variables			
Mother's standard of obedience	34.5	*ns*	
Amount of mother's affection-ate demonstration	43.5	*ns*	
Amount of time mother plays with child	33.0	*ns*	
Warmth, mother to child	33.0	*ns*	
Frequency with which *mother* spanks	32.0	.14*	Lows=spanked more frequently
Family climate variables			
Praise for good behavior at table	40.5	*ns*	

Strictness about bedtime	35.0	*ns*	
Strictness about noise	19.0	.025	Lows=parents more strict
Restrictions on physical mobility	40.5	*ns*	
Amount of praise for obedience	32.0	.14*	Highs=praised more
Amount of attention child wants	31.5	*ns*	
Sex role differentiation	45.0	*ns*	
Permissiveness for aggression toward parents	37.5	*ns*	
Punishment for aggression toward parents	36.5	*ns*	
Extent of use of tangible rewards	43.0	*ns*	
Extent of use of praise	18.0	.01–.025	Highs=praise used more often
Parents' agreement on child-rearing policies	33.0	*ns*	
Responsibility for child-rearing policies	30.5	.12*	Highs=father has more responsibility
Division of labor between husband and wife	23.0	.05	Highs=less division of labor
Conscience development variables			
Spontaneous telling of deviations	30.5	.12*	Highs=tell more often
Does child admit deviations when asked	12.5	.001–.01	Highs=admit to deviations
Evidence of conscience development	26.0	.05–.10	Highs=more evidence of conscience

*p values estimated by the Z transformation method (23).

Father-Son Relationships

As Table 1 indicates, the high and low masculinity groups differed in a number of familial variables. The data of the present study, like those of earlier ones (13, 15, 21), show that sex-typing of interests is more directly related to boys' interactions with their fathers than with their mothers. While none of the variables pertaining to mother-son relationships significantly differentiated the two groups, several of the variables of father-son interaction did. The differences were most clear-cut in two variables: (a) the highly masculine boys and their fathers were rated as "acting more affectionately toward each other"; and (b) the father-to-child affectional bonds are stronger in the case of the boys in this group.

These findings clearly lend support to the developmental identification hypothesis. They confirm the prediction, based on that hypothesis, that young boys are more likely to identify strongly with their fathers, and thus to acquire appropriately sex-typed responses, if their relationships with them are rewarding, warm, and affectionate.

Some additional trends in the data suggest that, if the father plays a very active role in his son's upbringing, the boy is more likely to develop strong masculine identification. Thus, compared with the fathers of the low masculine group, the fathers of highly masculine sons tended to take care of their sons more frequently and to have greater responsibility for the family's child-rearing policies. While these differences between the groups were not statistically significant, the findings suggest that the degree of the young boy's masculinity is related to the frequency and intensity of his contacts with his father and to the latter's influence in determining how the child is handled.

These trends, together with the significant findings about the warmth and affection of the fathers of highly masculine boys, may also be interpreted as evidence supportive of the role-taking hypothesis of identification. According to this hypothesis, a boy will be most strongly motivated to identify with his father, or, in role theory terms, to imitate him or take on his role, if he has intensive interactions with that parent and regards him as having a great deal of power. Predictions derived from this hypothesis appear to be confirmed by these data. Thus, it seems reasonable to infer that, since they are warm and affectionate, the fathers of highly masculine boys interact more frequently and more intensively with their sons. Therefore, these boys have more experience in practicing their appropriate sex roles. Moreover, since these fathers tend to take care of their sons often and, to a great extent, determine the techniques of disciplining the child, they do, in fact, have a great deal of power over the child, i.e., they can control his rewards and punishments. In short, these data seem to be consistent with the role-taking, as well as the developmental, hypothesis of identification.

None of the data of this study support the hypothesis of defensive identification, which maintains that high masculine identification is a consequence of the father being threatening and punitive. Ratings of the father's standards of obedience for the child, his frequency of spanking, and his strictness, based on the mothers' reports, did not significantly differentiate the high and low masculinity groups.

Family Climate

There is some evidence that, in addition to experiencing different kinds of father-son relationships, the two groups also encounter different general home atmospheres. Compared with the other group, the families of the highly masculine boys appeared to be more permissive, easygoing, more love-oriented, and less punitive in their disciplinary techniques. More specifically, as Table 1 indicates, the families of the highly masculine boys were less strict about noise in the home and more frequently used praise as a technique of discipline.

Other trends in the data give further support to these statistically significant findings. Highly masculine boys tended to be spanked less by their mothers and to get less praise for obedience. Since these boys' parents make more use of praise generally, their tendency to use less praise specifically for obedience may indicate that they place relatively less emphasis on this characteristic and thus maintain less strict, more permissive home atmospheres.

Moreover, the highly masculine boys tended to be less

attention-seeking—and, by inference, less dependent—than their peers who were relatively low in masculinity. Interpreted in the light of findings of other studies, this may indicate that the high group experiences more maternal nurturance (22), less maternal rejection, and less punishment for dependency (20). While it must be emphasized that these last findings represent suggestive trends rather than statistically significant differences between groups, they give some further evidence that appropriate sex-typing is fostered by a warm and permissive familial milieu.

One other familial variable, division of labor between husband and wife, significantly differentiated the two groups. According to mothers' reports, the families of the highly masculine-identified boys are characterized by fewer specifically "mother" and "father" tasks and a greater tendency for each parent to help with all tasks. The relative paucity of rules regarding duties may be another reflection of the relaxed climate of the home of the highly identified child. It may also indicate a generally harmonious family situation in which the parents can depend on each other's assistance without regulations about assignments. As Mowrer (12) has suggested, in the harmonious family both parents are likely to reward the boy's imitation of his father. Thus, both encourage the boy to identify with his father and in this way promote the development of a high degree of masculinity.

Conscience Development

If, as is generally assumed, appropriate sex-typing and high conscience development are both products of the process of parental identification, it would be predicted that independent measures of these two variables would be related. The findings confirm this prediction and thus support the underlying assumption. As may be seen in Table 1, highly masculine boys were rated higher than boys low in masculinity in measures of conscience development. More specifically, the former group received higher ratings in the variables, "admitting deviations when asked" and "evidence of conscience development," an over-all rating of superego. Moreover, there was a tendency for the highly masculine to be rated higher on the variable "tells about deviation," which referred to the child's proneness to confess wrong-doing spontaneously.

DISCUSSION

The interpretation of the findings is somewhat complicated by the fact that the data were derived exclusively from mothers' reports of their own and the fathers' behavior. The data on fathers' attitudes and general family climate may therefore be confounded. For example, reports that the fathers of highly masculine boys are affectionate might be a function of the mothers' view of the family climate as warm and permissive, rather than a specific commentary on the fathers' behavior. Nevertheless, the results of the present study are consistent with other empirical findings and with developmental and role theories of identification. The authors have previously reported that highly masculine kindergarten boys perceive their fathers as warm, nurturant, and rewarding (13), and the data of the present study suggest that, at least according to the mothers' replies, these fathers' overt behavior is characteristically affectionate. The consistency of the findings from two independently derived sets of data supports the validity of the developmental hypothesis of identification.

The present findings may also be interpreted as lending support to the role theory of identification. If the fathers of highly masculine boys are in fact more affectionate, they probably interact frequently and intensely with their sons. Furthermore, they tend to be influential in determining child-rearing policies and hence probably exercise considerable power over the boys. These two characteristics of the father—a high level of interaction with the son and great power over him—are, according to role theory, the primary prerequisites of the boy's strong identification with him.

The present data indicate that highly masculine boys live in relatively permissive, nonpunitive family climates. It seems plausible to infer that boys in such families are happier and more relaxed in their relationships with their parents than boys from stricter homes. Under these circumstances they are likely to seek frequent contact with their parents and to be relatively uninhibited in trying out many imitative responses in their presence. Responses that are appropriately sex-typed will be rewarded and hence will gain in habit strength, while inappropriate responses will not be rewarded and thus will be weakened or extinguished. In a stricter, more rigid home the child may tend to withdraw from his parents and, for this reason, will have less opportunity to learn which responses are most appropriate to his sex role.

While the findings based on mothers' reports of father-son relations and family climate were generally congruent with those discovered in the analysis of children's perceptions of their families, the two sets of data yielded different results for variables pertaining to father punishment and threat potential. Differences in the doll play responses of boys high and low in masculinity tended to support the defensive identification hypothesis, i.e., the former *perceived* their fathers as more punitive and threatening (13). According to the mothers' reports, however, the fathers of highly masculine boys did not *behave* more punitively or threateningly toward their sons than the fathers of boys low in masculinity. The data of the present study thus lend no support to the defensive identification hypothesis. There are no data that enable us to determine whether the child's or the mother's perceptions are more in accord with reality. The highly masculine boys' perceptions of their fathers may be related to the fact that these boys interact more with their fathers, and, consequently, in their doll play use the father dolls more prominently as agents of both nurturance and punishment. Thus, the threatening qualities attributed to the fathers in doll play may reflect, not their actual behavior, but their salience in the lives of their sons. On the other hand, it is equally possible that these fathers actually are, or have been, severe in their treatment of their sons. The mothers, however, viewing their husbands as affectionate toward their sons, may be unwilling or unable to admit the punitive aspects of the fathers' behavior. The problem can probably be solved only by systematic observations of father-son interactions among those high and low in masculinity.

Another finding of the study—the association between high degrees of masculinity in boys, assumed to be a manifestation of strong father identification and highly developed conscience, the index of identification used by Sears, Maccoby, and Levin (20)—merits discussion. Both measures have been found to be related to the high use of praise by parents and, more generally, to the use of love-oriented techniques of discipline. However, warmth and acceptance by the mother and acceptance by the father were found to be antecedents of a high degree of conscience development in kindergarten boys (20), while the father's warmth and affection, not the mother's, were found to be related to masculinity in boys this age. On theoretical and empirical grounds, it is reasonable to consider both conscience development and masculinity as signs of identification, but the two characteristics appear to have different correlates or antecedents.

In the process of ego and superego development the child undoubtedly has not one, but a number of identification models. Different aspects of his psychological structure become modeled after different identificands. Thus, for the five-year-old boy both parents probably serve as models for conscience development; that is, his moral values and ethical standards are products of identifications with his mother *and* father.[2] If this is true, then, according to the developmental identification hypothesis, a high degree of conscience development would depend upon positive affectional relationships between the child and *both* parents. Viewed in this way, association between the boy's high level of conscience and both his parents' acceptance and warmth (20) was to be anticipated. The same finding may also be interpreted as confirmation of a prediction based on role theory. Insofar as warm and affectionate parents interact more with their children, these children would be expected to identify strongly with them, to adopt more of their characteristics, and, consequently, to develop strong conscience.

The boy's adoption of masculine interests, on the other hand, must be almost exclusively the product of his identification with his father, for he is the parent who serves as the model for masculinity. Since the mother obviously cannot be the model for this, her role in her son's acquisition of masculine characteristics cannot be as vital as the father's. Therefore, according to the

[2]It is, of course, possible that ultimately the boy's conscience will be modeled primarily after his father's, but during the preschool period his standards are more likely to be adopted from both parents.

developmental identification hypothesis, appropriate sex-typing for the boy is a consequent of warm and affectionate interactions with his father, while his relationships with his mother are less important in this respect. Analogously, according to role theory, the amount and intensity of father-son, but not mother-son, interactions determine the masculinity of the boy's behavior and interests. The data of this study substantiate this reasoning. High degrees of masculinity were in fact fostered by affectionate— and, by inference, frequent and intense—father-son interactions, but were not significantly affected by mother-son relationships.

Summary

The mothers of 19 boys, nine of them high and ten of them low in masculinity as measured by the IT Scale, were interviewed about their own and their husbands' child-rearing practices and the boys' conscience development. On the basis of these interviews ratings were made on 28 variables of father-son relationships, family climate, and conscience.

The major findings were as follows:

1. The variables of father-son relationships are more directly associated with sex-typing than are those pertaining to mother-son relations.

2. According to mothers' reports the fathers of the highly masculine group had stronger affectional bonds, and acted more affectionately, toward their sons than did the fathers of boys low in masculinity. These findings appear to support the developmental hypothesis of identification.

3. There were trends in the data that suggest that the fathers of the highly masculine group play a greater role in their son's upbringing, doing more of their sons' caretaking and having greater responsibility for child-rearing policies. These trends, together with the findings about the warmth and affection of the fathers of highly masculine boys, may be interpreted as supportive of the role theory of identification.

4. The highly masculine boys appear to experience more permissive, easygoing familial climate and less punitive, more

love-oriented techniques of discipline than their less masculine peers.

5. Boys high in masculinity tend to be high in conscience development, too. The correlates of these two products of parental identification are quite different, however.

REFERENCES

1. Brim, O. G., Jr. 1958. Family structure and sex role learning by children: A further analysis of Helen Koch's data. *Sociometry* 21: 1–16.
2. Bronfenbrenner, U. 1958. The study of identification through interpersonal perception. In R. Tagiuri and L. Petrullo (eds.), *Person perception and interpersonal behavior.* Stanford: Stanford University Press. Pp. 110–30.
3. Brown, D. G. 1956. Sex role preference in young children. *Psychological Monographs* 70, no. 14 (whole no. 421).
4. Cava, E. L., and H. L. Raush. 1952. Identification and the adolescent boy's perception of his father. *Journal of Abnormal and Social Psychology* 47: 855–56.
5. Cottrell, L. S., Jr. 1942. The analysis of situational fields in social psychology. *American Sociological Review* 7: 370–83.
6. Freud, Anna. 1937. *The ego and the mechanisms of defense.* London: Hogarth Press.
7. Freud, S. 1933. The passing of the Oedipus-complex. In *Collected papers,* vol. II. London: Hogarth Press. Pp. 269–82.
8. Freud, S. 1936. *The problem of anxiety.* New York: Norton.
9. Freud, S. 1949. *Group psychology and the analysis of the ego.* London: Hogarth Press.
10. Levin, H., and R. R. Sears. 1956. Identification with parents as a determinant of doll play aggression. *Child Development* 27: 135–53.
11. Mann, H. B., and D. R. Whitney. 1947. On a test of whether one of two random variables is stochastically larger than the other. *Annals of Mathematical Statistics* 18: 50–60.
12. Mowrer, O. H. 1950. *Learning theory and personality dynamics.* New York: Ronald Press.
13. Mussen P., and L. Distler. 1959. Masculinity, identification, and father-son relationships. *Journal of Abnormal and Social Psychology* 59: 350–56.
14. Parsons, T. 1955. Family structure and the socialization of the child. In T. Parsons and R. F. Bales (eds.), *Family, socialization, and interaction process.* Glencoe, Ill.: Free Press. Pp. 35–131.
15. Payne, D. E., and P. H. Mussen. 1956. Parent-child relationships and father identification among adolescent boys. *Journal of Abnormal and Social Psychology* 52: 358–62.
16. Richards, T. W., and Marjorie Simons. 1941. Fels Child Behavior Scale. *Genetic Psychological Monograph* 24: 259–309.
17. Sanford, N. 1955. The dynamics of identification. *Psychological Review* 62: 106–17.
18. Sears, Pauline. 1953. Child-rearing factors related to playing of sex-typed roles. *American Psychologist* 8: 431. (Abstract)

19. Sears, R. R. 1951. A theoretical framework for personality and social behavior. *American Psychologist* 6: 476–82.
20. Sears, R. R.; Eleanor E. Maccoby; and H. Levin. 1957. *Patterns of child rearing.* Evanston, Ill.: Row, Peterson.
21. Sears, R. R.; M. H. Pintler; and Pauline Sears. 1946. Effect of father separation on preschool children's doll play aggression. *Child Development* 17: 219–43.
22. Sears, R. R.; J. W. M. Whiting; V. Nowles; and Pauline Sears. 1953. Some child-rearing antecedents of aggression and dependency in young children. *Genetic Psychological Monograph* 47: 135–234.
23. Siegel, S. 1956. *Nonparametric statistics.* New York: McGraw-Hill.
24. Sopchak, A. 1952. Parental "identification" and "tendency toward disorders" as measured by the MMPI. *Journal of Abnormal and Social Psychology* 47: 159–65.

6

*Patterning of Parental Affection
and Disciplinary Dominance
as a Determinant of Guilt
and Sex Typing*

ROBERT W. MOULTON,
EUGENE BURSTEIN,
PAUL G. LIBERTY, JR.,
and NATHAN ALTUCHER

Both the development of conscience, as evidenced in guilt or turning aggression against the self (Sears, 1960), and sex typing (Kagan, 1964) are presumed to reflect the internalization of or identification with parental attributes. (For extended discussions of the issues attending the "identification" concept, see Becker, 1964; Bronfenbrenner, 1960; Heilbrun, 1965.) Research on the child-rearing antecedents of these characteristics has tended to

Robert W. Moulton, Eugene Burnstein, Paul G. Liberty, Jr., and Nathan Altucher, "Patterning of Parental Affection and Disciplinary Dominance as a Determinant of Guilt and Sex Typing," *Journal of Personality and Social Psychology* 4, no. 4 (1966): 356–63. Copyright 1966 by the American Psychological Association, and reproduced by permission. Footnotes have been renumbered.

focus *either* on parent-child affectional relationships *or* on the nature of disciplinary interactions. However, results from several studies suggest that attention must be given to the *patterning* of these two classes of variables (e.g., LeVine, 1961; Mussen & Distler, 1959; Unger, 1962). An often cited finding reported by Sears, Maccoby, and Levin (1957) is a good example of evidence pointing to the need for such refinements in design and analysis. They show that the use of withdrawal of love as a disciplinary technique was related to indexes of conscience development only when used by a parent rated as generally warm in relationships with the child.

One of the clearest theoretical arguments for a systematic consideration of the patterning of disciplinary and affectional behavior is found in the writings of Henry and Short (1954). These authors state that internalization of parental characteristics, as evidenced in guilt and aggression against the self, is most likely to occur when the parent who is perceived to be the major source of threat or frustration is also seen as an important source of affection. Under these circumstances, the child is likely to inhibit aggression against the source of frustration because not to do so would jeopardize the gratifications received in this affectionate relationship. A common recourse is to turn aggression inward and, given these circumstances, self-blame and guilt are likely to become predominant modes of expression of aggression. In other family situations where the major source of frustration does not at the same time represent an important source of affection, aggression is not likely to jeopardize affectionate gratification. Because this particular deterrent to the overt expression is absent, aggression turned outward is likely to become a predominant mode of expression. Since the mother, in accordance with her cultural role, is usually the parent who represents the most important source of affection, Henry and Short (1954) reason that when she is the dominant disciplinarian, and thus the major source of frustration, turning aggression

This research was supported by grants from the Department of Education, University of California, Berkeley, to the first-named author; National Science Foundation Contract GS-570 to the second author; and the 6570th Personnel Research Laboratory, Aerospace Medical Division AFSC Project 7719(02), to the third author. During some of the work, the third author held a research fellowship from the National Institute of Health, United States Public Health Service.

against the self and consequent strong guilt are likely. This argument can account for some of the relevant findings. For example, King and Henry (1955) observed that adult males who report that their mothers had been dominant in discipline show a cardiovascular reaction under stress which in previous research had been demonstrated to be characteristic of guilty or depressed individuals. Heinicke (1953) reports that when the mother and not the father was the dominant disciplinarian guilt was high in 5-year-old boys.

On the other hand, Sears (1961) offers evidence that "self-aggression" among 12-year-old boys was related to a clear assumption of disciplinary functions by the father when the child was 5 years old. Sears also reports other findings in the same paper which not only provide a means of resolving the apparent inconsistencies, but also reemphasize the need to take into account the patterning of discipline and affection. Sears found that among fathers who were the chief disciplinarians and who were strict, only those who were also "warm" had sons with high self-aggression scores.

An implication of this group of findings is that the position taken by Henry and Short (1954) should be expanded to include the possibility that *either* parent may be an important source of affection and that strong internalization will result whenever the dominant disciplinarian, whether it is the mother or the father, is also an important source of affection.

The first part of the study being reported represents an attempt to provide a test of these arguments through examination of the degree to which introspective reports of the frequency and ease of arousal of guilt (which were used as an index of the degree of internalization of parental standards) can be predicted from the patterning of parental affectional and disciplinary behaviors as reported by young adult males. On the basis of responses to questionnaire items, subjects were classified with respect to guilt, and it was determined which parent was seen as having been dominant in discipline and whether each parent was seen as high or low in affection.

Given such data, certain problems in analysis must be recognized. It is expected that when the dominant disciplinarian is high in affection, guilt will be high, while when the dominant disciplinarian is low in affection, guilt will be low. However, the subjects for whom the dominant disciplinarian is high in affection include all subjects for whom both parents are affectionate and part of the group for whom at least one parent is affectionate. Thus differences in guilt between individuals for whom the dominant disciplinarian was high or low in affection might simply reflect the fact that when the dominant disciplinarian was high in affection, the child received more affection from parents in general (the gross affection hypothesis). There are several ways to deal with this problem. First, if variations in affection provided by the dominant disciplinarian show a stronger relationship to guilt than do variations in affection provided by the nondominant disciplinarian, then clearly it is the combination of affection and dominance and not simply the total amount of affection which is important.

Second, according to "patterning" hypotheses we would anticipate that individuals with two parents high in affection will not show a greater frequency of high guilt than will those with just one high-affectionate parent *if* the affectionate parent is also the dominant disciplinarian. Similarly, those for whom the one affectionate parent is not the dominant disciplinarian will not show a greater frequency of high guilt than subjects for whom neither parent is high in affection. The "gross affection" hypothesis would lead to quite different predictions.

A second aspect of the study being reported is an attempt to examine sex-typed responses as these relate to reports of parental characteristics. To the extent that the identification process, which is presumed to mediate the relationships between certain parental behaviors and guilt discussed above, involves a literal modeling of parental traits by the child, it should be possible to predict the child's sex-typed responses on the basis of a knowledge of the patterning of these same parental characteristics. Such reasoning is consistent with findings from several past investigations. Payne and Mussen (1956) note that adolescent boys who see the father as warm, according to projective test responses, were more likely to perceive themselves as similar to the father. Likewise, Bandura and Walters (1959) report an association between the father's rated warmth and the son's feeling of similarity to the father. With respect to dominance in discipline, Altucher (1956) has shown that appropriately sex-identified boys report that the father was dominant in discipline, while more feminine boys report that the mother was the dominant disciplinarian. Clearly relevant to the patterning hypothesis, Mussen and Distler (1959) show that young boys who were categorized as "masculine" were more likely than boys categorized as feminine to perceive their fathers as important sources of nurturance *and* of punishment.

Thus, in the present study it is anticipated that the subject's sex typing will correspond more closely to the sex of the dominant disciplinarian when the latter is also high in affection than when he is low in affection. Similarly, variations in the amount of affection afforded by the nondominant disciplinarian will not be as closely related to sex typing as are variations in the affection afforded by the dominant disciplinarian. Moreover, it will be especially important to show that the relationships hold regardless of whether the dominant disciplinarian is the mother or the father. More specifically, under conditions in which the father is dominant, the son should be more likely to show masculine sex typing if the father is high in affection than if he is low. Mother's affection should not be so closely related to sex typing as father's affection for father-dominated subjects. An analogous set of predictions are made for mother-dominanted subjects.

PROCEDURE

Subjects were male students enrolled in three large sections of introductory psychology at a state university. Participation in the study was a course requirement, and 99 per cent (N=176) of the males enrolled in these sections participated. A questionnaire was administered, and on the basis of responses to relevant items (described below) subjects were classified with respect to the variables of guilt, sex typing, parental affection, and parental dominance. In 15 cases, a parent had been absent for an extended period during the subject's childhood, and these individuals were eliminated from the sample.

Guilt and Sex Typing

Guilt. This variable was assessed through multiple-choice items as follows:

> 1. How often would you say that you feel guilty? *(a)* once a day or more, *(b)* once a week, *(c)* once a month, *(d)* every few months, *(e)* once a year or less.
> 2. How easy is it for something to make you feel guilty? *(a)* very easy, *(b)* easy, *(c)* difficult, *(d)* very difficult.
> 3. When was the last time you can remember feeling guilty? *(a)* within the past day, *(b)* a few days ago, *(c)* more than a week ago, *(d)* more than a month ago, *(e)* more than a year ago.

A numerical score was assigned for responses to each of these items, and these scores were summed for each subject. The resulting distribution was divided at the median to provide high- and low-guilt groups.

The validity of a self-report measure of guilt is supported by several previous studies which indicated that simple direct questioning with regard to this characteristic yielded a measure related in expected ways to other indexes of strength of internalization (Bandura & Walters, 1959; MacKinnon, 1938; Moulton, 1957). However, as a further check on the validity of this means of measuring guilt, a number of open-ended questions were asked about the individual's guilt reaction. Judges were asked to read these responses without knowledge of other responses of the subject and to code for the presence or absence of the kinds of expiatory behavior expected of persons subject to strong guilt reactions. Some of the respondents reported self-denying, self-punishing responses, confession, or some other active attempt to reduce the intensity or duration of the guilt reaction. Others showed no particular indication that they found it necessary to carry out maneuvers of this kind in response to guilt feelings. Judges were able to sort subjects into two groups on the basis of the frequency of these responses with a high level of interjudge agreement (87 per cent). Among high-guilt subjects as selected by their responses to the objective items, 84 per cent were characterized by active attempts to relieve guilt feelings, while among low-guilt subjects, only 20 per cent reported such ameliorative activities. The two ratings of guilt thus showed considerable overlap.

Sex typing. A modified version of a measure of sex typing, devised by Gough (1952), was used in the present study. Scores were divided at the median to provide groups categorized as masculine or feminine. It was assumed for purposes of this study that a "masculine" score on this measure represents evidence that strength of identification with the father is relatively greater than strength of identification with the mother, while a "feminine" score indicates the opposite state of affairs. Difficulties in making such an assumption have been pointed to by Bronfenbrenner (1958) and others. However, the successful use of the modified Gough measure by Altucher (1956) in a previous study of the antecedents of sex typing suggests that this instrument is valid for purposes of this study.

Socialization Variables

Socialization variables were assessed through reports on parental characteristics provided by subjects. Several studies provide evidence as to the accuracy of such reports on parental attributes similar to the ones in the present study. Bronson, Katten, and Livson (1959) gathered reports concerned with parental affection and authority from children. The children's reports were compared to data on these parental behaviors obtained from several other sources. The correspondence between these reports was relatively high, and the authors conclude that, on the whole, children are accurate in their representation of these parental behaviors. Kohn and Clausen (1956) interviewed adult schizophrenic patients in an attempt to determine the patterning of dominance and affection which characterized their parents. Hospital case records were examined, and, where possible, a sibling or other close relative was interviewed. Judgments about these parental characteristics obtained from independent sources were highly related to the reports obtained from the patients. Thus reports on aspects of parental behaviors relevant to the present study appear to be usefully accurate estimates of the actual situation in the home.

Parental affection. It was assumed that a parent who was an important source of affection would be perceived to have been a readily available source of positive interaction. Activities were selected which seemed relatively easy to recall and provided an index of the extent to which the parent responded to requests for positive interaction. Ten items of the following representative types were employed: (1) I could interrupt my father (mother) when he was with others, (2) My father (mother) took me with him when he ran errands. The items were to be answered by checking "always," "often," "sometimes," "rarely," or "never." Numerical scores on these items were summed for each parent, and the resulting distributions were divided at the median. Each parent was in this way designated as high or low in affection.

Dominance in discipline. The items used to assess this characteristic were similar to those used in a previous investigation (Altucher, 1956) dealing with sex typing and parental dominance. For each of five items, the subject could respond "mother," "father," "neither," or "both." The items were:

1. Who disciplined you if you did something wrong that was serious?
2. If there was some question as to whether your conduct was right or wrong, who decided?
3. Whose discipline did you fear the most?
4. Who disciplined you when you disobeyed?
5. Whose discipline was most effective?

If the number of items checked as "mother" equaled or exceeded the number of items checked as "father," the subject was designated as mother dominated, and those for whom the number of items checked as "father" exceeded the number checked as "mother" were placed in the father-dominated group. This method placed 42 of the subjects in the mother-dominated group and 101 in the father-dominated group. Eight subjects answered all of these items "both" or "neither," and were eliminated from the sample for these analyses.

RESULTS

The relationships between our measures of guilt, sex typing, parental affection, and disciplinary dominance were subjected to chi-square tests. The analyses relevant to guilt are summarized in Tables 1 and 2. It can be seen from Table 1 (Comparison 1) that disciplinary dominance alone is not related to guilt, though there is a slight tendency for mother dominance to be associated with high guilt ($p < .20$).[1] As predicted, however, variations in affection afforded by the dominant disciplinarian are strongly related to guilt ($p < .001$; Comparison 2, Table 1), while the relationship

TABLE 1
GUILT AS RELATED TO PARENTAL DOMINANCE
AND PARENTAL AFFECTION

Comparisons	N	High guilt	Low guilt	χ^2
1. Mother dominant	43	25	18	
Father dominant	110	50	60	1.99*
2. Dominant disciplinarian				
High affection	85	57	28	
Low affection	68	18	50	24.90**
3. Nondominant Disciplinarian				
High affection	74	36	38	
Low affection	79	39	40	1.00
4. Father-dominant Ss				
High father affection	61	37	24	
Low father affection	49	13	36	15.95**
5. Father-dominant Ss				
High mother affection	55	24	31	
Low mother affection	55	26	29	1.00
6. Mother-dominant Ss				
High mother affection	24	20	4	
Low mother affection	19	5	14	11.92**
7. Mother-dominant Ss				
High father affection	19	12	7	
Low father affection	24	13	11	1.00

*$p < .20$.
**$p < .001$.

[1]All probability values are based on the two-tailed test. The correction for continuity was used when an expected frequency fell below 10.

between the amount of affection provided by the nondominant disciplinarian and guilt does not approach significance (Comparison 3, Table 1). Note also that for father-dominated subjects there is a significant positive relationship between father's affection and guilt ($p < .0001$; Comparison 4, Table 1). However, Mother's affection and guilt are not significantly related in the father-dominated group (Comparison 5, Table 1). In the mother-dominated group, mother's affection is positively related to guilt ($p < .001$; Comparison 6, Table 1), while father's affection is not significantly related to guilt for the mother-dominated subjects (Comparison 7, Table 1)

In Table 2, subjects were classified into three groups according to whether one, both, or neither parent was reported to be high in affection. It can be seen that low guilt occurs frequently when both parents are low in affection. By inspection, it would appear that having two affectionate parents does not produce high guilt with any appreciably greater frequency than having just one affectionate parent. However, note the relative distribution of guilt among subjects who had just one affectionate parent. As can be seen in Table 2, high guilt is much more frequent among subjects for whom the one affectionate parent is also the dominant disciplinarian than among those for whom the one affectionate parent is not the dominant disciplinarian ($p < .001$). Thus, the presence of one affectionate parent is not associated with high guilt unless the affectionate parent is also the dominant disciplinarian.

An interesting trend can be noted from the data in Table 2. High guilt was expected for subjects for whom both parents were affectionate because under these circumstances the dominant disciplinarian must be affectionate. High guilt was also expected, of course, when just one parent was affectionate if the affectionate parent was also the dominant disciplinarian. The percentage of high guilt under the latter condition (79 per cent) actually exceeds the percentage of high guilt under the former condition (60 per cent). The difference approaches significance ($\chi^2 = 3.36$, $p < .10$). This tentative difference will be dealt with in the discussion.

Results of the analyses of the data on sex typing are presented in Tables 3 and 4. There is a statistically significant tendency for sex typing to correspond to the sex of the dominant

TABLE 2

GROSS AFFECTION VERSUS PATTERNING OF AFFECTION AND DISCIPLINE
AS RELATED TO GUILT

Gross affection	Guilt			Patterning of affection and discipline	Guilt		
	High	Low	N		High	Low	N
Both parents high in affection	31	21	52	Dominant parent high in affection, nondominant parent low in affection	26	7	33
1 parent high, 1 parent low in affection	31	24	55	Dominant parent low in affection, nondominant parent high in affection	5	17	22
Both parents low in affection	13	33	46	Total	31	24	55
Total	75	78	153				

Note.—For Gross affection, $\chi^2(2) = 11.50$, $p < .01$. For Patterning of affection and discipline, $\chi^2 = 14.67$, $p < .001$.

disciplinarian. Sons with dominant mothers tend to be feminine, and sons with dominant fathers tend to be masculine ($p < .01$; Comparison 1, Table 3). However, as expected, subject's sex typing corresponds more closely to the sex of the dominant disciplinarian when the dominant disciplinarian is high in affection than when he is low ($p < .01$; Table 4). Note that when the dominant disciplinarian is low in affection, sex typing of the son shows no particular tendency to correspond to the sex of the dominant disciplinarian. Thus dominance alone in the absence of high affection does not seem to produce a correspondence between son's sex typing and the sex of the dominant disciplinarian. Moreover, it can be seen from Table 4 that variations in affection afforded by the nondominant disciplinarian are not significantly related ($p < .20$) to the extent to which sex typing tended to correspond to the sex of the latter.

The impact on sex typing of a combination of affection and dominance is important for both mother and father. In Table 3 (Comparison 2) it is seen that when the father is dominant and

TABLE 3

MASCULINITY-FEMININITY AS RELATED TO PARENTAL
DOMINANCE AND PARENTAL AFFECTION

Comparisons	N	Mas-culine	Femi-nine	χ^2
1. All *S*s				
Mother dominant	43	14	29	
Father dominant	110	64	46	8.12***
2. Father-dominant *S*s				
High father affection	61	40	21	
Low father affection	49	24	25	3.08*
3. Mother-dominant *S*s				
High mother affection	24	4	20	
Low mother affection	19	10	9	4.72**
4. Father-dominant *S*s				
High mother affection	55	30	25	
Low mother affection	55	34	21	1.00
5. Mother-dominant *S*s				
High father affection	19	8	11	
Low father affection	24	6	18	1.00

  *$p < .10$.
  **$p < .05$.
  ***$p < .01$.

TABLE 4
RELATIONSHIPS BETWEEN AFFECTION LEVEL OF
DOMINANT AND NONDOMINANT DISCIPLINARIANS
AND DEGREE TO WHICH SUBJECT'S SEX TYPING
CORRESPONDS TO SEX OF DISCIPLINARIAN

Groups compared	S's sex typing corresponds to sex of disciplinarian			
	N	Yes	No	χ^2
Dominant disciplinarian				
High affection	85	60	25	6.76**
Low affection	68	34	34	
Nondominant disciplinarian				
High affection	74	33	41	1.74*
Low affection	79	27	52	

*$p < .20$.
**$p < .01$.

high in affection, masculinity is more frequent than when he is
dominant but not high in affection, though this finding does not
reach the conventionally acceptable level of statistical significance ($p < .10$). Analogously, high affection in a dominant
mother increases femininity ($p < .05$, Comparison 3, Table 3).
Note also that variations in affection afforded by the mother are
not significantly associated with sex typing among father-
dominated subjects (Comparison 4, Table 3) and that father's
affection is not related to sex typing among mother-dominated
subjects (Comparison 5, Table 3).

DISCUSSION

The present study supports Henry and Short (1954) by
demonstrating that the development of strong guilt reactions
depends on a combination of affection and disciplinary dominance in one parent. It extends their analysis by observing that
the association between guilt and the affection-disciplinary pattern is independent of which parent combines these characteristics.

As a conjecture, the findings with regard to guilt suggest a
general principle. Any system of socialization which is arranged

so that the child becomes dependent on a continued flow of affection and in which a continued supply of affection is contingent on conformity to demands is likely to produce strong internalization. Factors which reduce the degree of dependency on any one source of affection and/or reduce the extent to which receipt of affection is consistently contingent on conformity to demands will reduce the extent to which a given socialization system produces strong internalization. For example, when affection is available from more than one source, the possibility of enforcing demands through threats to withdraw affection is reduced because of the possibility of obtaining affection from another source as an alternative to complying with demands. Thus, even if the dominant disciplinarian and the other parent were both high in affection, the possibility of turning to the nondominant disciplinarian for affection rather than conforming to the demands of the dominant disciplinarian would always be present. This kind of analysis might account for the tentative observation that the frequency of high guilt among subjects with two parents high in affection was somewhat less than that found among those with just one parent high in affection, but who at the same time was the dominant disciplinarian.

It should be pointed out, however, that the impact of alternative sources of affection may be counteracted if demands from the various individuals who provide affection are clearly coordinated and consistent. Thus Bandura and Walters (1959) and Peck (1958) find that well-socialized children tend to come from homes in which parents approve of and support each other's disciplinary efforts. At the other extreme, a lack of coordination or consistency between parental demands should clearly tend to reduce the extent to which receipt of affection is clearly contingent on conforming to demands, and a very low degree of internalization would be expected. Several studies (Bandura & Walters, 1959; Glueck & Glueck, 1950) have shown that just this lack of coordination characterizes the families of antisocial delinquents.

Certain social conditions may increase the likelihood that affection and discipline will be focused in one parent. Absence of the father is an obvious case in point which has received some study. If it can be assumed that guilt and the degree of overt aggressiveness are negatively related, as previous writings have suggested (Bandura & Walters, 1959; MacKinnon, 1938; Moulton, 1957), then the present findings may have implications for studies of the relationship between father absence and son's aggressive behavior. Reasoning from the formulation suggested in the present paper, absence of the father might tend to increase the extent to which affection and discipline will be focused in one parent, and thus low aggressiveness would be expected in sons. Some studies have indeed found low aggressiveness in sons to be associated with father absence (Bach, 1946; Sears, Pintler, & Sears, 1946). This has previously been explained by assuming that father's absence means the child is likely to lack an aggressive role model. However, other research presents evidence that absence of the father is sometimes associated with a high incidence of antisocial, aggressive behavior (cf. Bacon, Child, & Barry, 1963; Burton & Whiting, 1961). Here an accounting is made in terms of the "reactive masculinity" of males whose "primary" identification is feminine. The formulation put forth in the present study suggests that the relationship between father absence and son's aggressive behavior will depend on the degree to which father absence is correlated with particular characteristics of the mother in the father-absent family. More specifically, assume that in certain populations fathers tend to be absent from families in which mothers are unable to provide a combination of affection and effective discipline. Thus, in sons of such father-absent families, aggression is high and internalization low. When fathers are absent from homes in which the mother does have the capacity to combine affection and effective discipline, then father absence may concentrate discipline and affection in the mother. In these families the sons should display high internalization and low aggression. This line of reasoning finds tentative support in recent research by McCord, McCord, and Thurber (1962). They observe that although, in general, father absence is associated with son's antisocial aggressiveness, mothers who were not "deviant" were able to raise sons who were relatively low in aggressiveness.

Let us consider some implications of the data on sex typing. It was shown that the son's sex typing corresponds more closely to the sex of the dominant disciplinarian when the latter was high

in affection, irrespective of which parent combined these characteristics. Assuming, as we have, that sex typing reflects relative
strength of identification with mother or father, the findings are
taken as evidence that a relatively strong identification is pro-
moted with the parent who combines affection and dominance.
Noting that it has been shown that the presence of such a parent
is also associated with the development of high guilt, it seems
plausible to interpret the results as supporting the idea that
internalized moral standards are acquired by means of an identification process and not simply as a reaction to the direct administration of rewards for "moral" behavior, as Hill (1960) and others
have argued (see Becker, 1964, for a review of this issue).

Finally, the findings suggest that some males develop a
strong set of internalized standards by modeling themselves after
the father and others by modeling after the mother. Thus it would
seem plausible to expect qualitative differences in the nature of
guilt-arousing incidents and in the kinds of expiatory behaviors
which characterize the two groups. Possibly the nature of internalized standards and guilt-produced behavior which result
from identification with a female would show a greater degree of
similarity to those typical of females than would the analogous
behaviors acquired through identification with a male. This seems
to be a clearly testable proposition and is an issue which should
be considered in studies of the effects of various family socialization patterns.

REFERENCES

Altucher, N. 1956. Conflict in sex identification in boys. Ph. D. dissertation. Ann
    Arbor: University of Michigan.
Bach, G. R. 1946. Father-fantasies and father-typing in father-separated children.
    Child Development 17: 63–80.
Bacon, M. K.; I. L. Child; and H. Barry. 1963. A cross-cultural study of correlates
    of crime. *Journal of Abnormal and Social Psychology* 66: 291–300.
Bandura, A., and R. H. Walters. 1959. *Adolescent aggression*. New York: Ronald
    Press.
Becker, W. C. 1964. Consequences of different kinds of parental discipline. In M.
    L. Hoffman and L. W. Hoffman (eds.), *Review of child development research*,
    vol. 1. New York: Russell Sage Foundation. Pp. 169–208.

Bronfenbrenner, U. 1958. The study of identification through interpersonal perception. In R. Taguiri and L. Petrullo (eds.), *Person perception and interpersonal behavior.* Stanford: Stanford University Press. Pp. 110–30.

Bronfenbrenner, U. 1960. Freudian theories of identification and their derivatives. *Child Development* 31: 15–40.

Bronson, W. C; E. S. Katten; and N. Livson. 1959. Patterns of authority and affection in two generations. *Journal of Abnormal and Social Psychology* 58: 143–52.

Burton, R. V., and J. W. M. Whiting. 1961. The absent father and cross-sex identity. *Merrill-Palmer Quarterly* 7: 85–95.

Glueck, S., and E. T. Glueck. 1950. *Unraveling juvenile delinquency.* Cambridge, Mass.: Harvard University Press.

Gough, H. G. 1952. Identifying psychological femininity. *Educational and Psychological Measurement* 12: 427–39.

Heilbrun, A. B., Jr. 1965. The measurement of identification. *Child Development* 36: 111–27.

Heinicke, C. M. 1953. Some antecedents and correlates of guilt and fear in young boys. Ph.D. dissertation. Cambridge, Mass.: Harvard University.

Henry, A. F., and J. F. Short. 1954. *Suicide and homicide.* Glencoe, Ill.: Free Press.

Hill, W. F. 1960. Learning theory and the acquisition of values. *Psychological Review* 67: 317–31.

Kagan, J. 1964. Acquisition and significance of sex typing and sex role identity. In M. L. Hoffman and L. W. Hoffman (eds.), *Review of child development research,* vol. 1. New York: Russell Sage Foundation. Pp. 137–67.

King, S., and A. Henry. 1955. Aggression and cardiovascular reactions related to parental control over behavior. *Journal of Abnormal and Social Psychology* 50: 206–10.

Kohn, M. L., and J. A. Clausen. 1956. Parental authority behavior and schizophrenia. *American Journal of Orthopsychiatry* 26: 297–313.

LeVine, B. B. 1961. Punishment techniques and the development of conscience. Ph.D. dissertation. Evanston, Ill.: Northwestern University.

MacKinnon, D. W. 1938. Violation of prohibitions. In H. W. Murray (ed.), *Explorations in personality.* New York: Oxford University Press. Pp. 491–501.

McCord, J.; W. McCord; and E. Thurber. 1962. Some effects of paternal absence on male children. *Journal of Abnormal and Social Psychology* 64: 361–69.

Moulton, R. W. 1957. Antecedents of aggressive expression in psychosis. PhD. dissertation. Ann Arbor: University of Michigan.

Mussen, P., and L. Distler. 1959. Masculinity, identification, and father-son relationships. *Journal of Abnormal and Social Psychology* 59: 350–56.

Payne, D., and P. Mussen. 1956. Parent-child relations and father identification among adolescent boys. *Journal of Abnormal and Social Psychology* 52: 358–62.

Peck, R. F. 1958. Family patterns correlated with adolescent personality structure. *Journal of Abnormal and Social Psychology* 57: 347–50.

Sears, R. R. 1960. The growth of conscience. In I. Iscoe and H. W. Stevenson (eds.), *Personality development in children.* Austin: University of Texas Press. Pp. 92–111.

Sears, R. R. 1961. Relation of early socialization experiences to aggression in middle childhood. *Journal of Abnormal and Social Psychology* 63: 466–92.

Sears, R. R.; E. E. Maccoby; and H. Levin. 1957. *Patterns of child rearing.*
    Evanston, Ill.: Row, Peterson.
Sears, R. R.; M. M. Pintler; and P. S. Sears. 1946. Effect of father separation on
    preschool children's doll play aggression. *Child Development* 17: 219–43.
Unger, S. M. 1962. Antecedents of personality differences in guilt responsitivity.
    Psychological Reports 10: 357–58.

III

Structural Effects

7

A Cross-Cultural Survey of Some Sex Differences in Socialization

HERBERT BARRY III,
MARGARET K. BACON,
and IRVIN L. CHILD

In our society, certain differences may be observed between the typical personality characteristics of the two sexes. These sex differences in personality are generally believed to result in part from differences in the way boys and girls are reared. To the extent that personality differences between the sexes are thus of cultural rather than biological origin, they seem potentially susceptible to change. But how readily susceptible to change? In the differential rearing of the sexes does our society make an arbitrary imposition on an infinitely plastic biological base, or is this cultural imposition found uniformly in all societies as an

Herbert Barry III, Margaret K. Bacon, and Irvin L. Child, "A Cross-Cultural Survey of Some Sex Differences in Socialization," *Journal of Abnormal and Social Psychology* 55 (November 1957): 327–32. Copyright 1957 by the American Psychological Association, and reproduced by permission. Footnotes have been renumbered.

adjustment to the real biological differences between the sexes? This paper reports one attempt to deal with this problem.

DATA AND PROCEDURES

The data used were ethnographic reports, available in the anthropological literature, about socialization practices of various cultures. One hundred and ten cultures, mostly nonliterate, were studied. They were selected primarily in terms of the existence of adequate ethnographic reports of socialization practices and secondarily so as to obtain a wide and reasonably balanced geographical distribution. Various aspects of socialization of infants and children were rated on a seven-point scale by two judges (Mrs. Bacon and Mr. Barry). Where the ethnographic reports permitted, separate ratings were made for the socialization of boys and girls. Each rating was indicated as either confident or doubtful; with still greater uncertainty, or with complete lack of evidence, the particular rating was of course not made at all. We shall restrict the report of sex difference ratings to cases in which both judges made a confident rating. Also omitted is the one instance where the two judges reported a sex difference in opposite directions, as it demonstrates only unreliability of judgment. The number of cultures that meet these criteria is much smaller than the total of 110; for the several variables to be considered, the number varies from 31 to 84.

The aspects of socialization on which ratings were made included:

1. Several criteria of attention and indulgence toward infants.

2. Strength of socialization from age four or five years until shortly before puberty, with respect to five systems of behavior; strength of socialization was defined as the combination of positive pressure (rewards for the behavior) plus negative pressure (punishments for lack of the behavior). The variables were:

(a) Responsibility or dutifulness training. (The data were such that training in the performance of chores in the productive or domestic economy was necessarily the principal source of information here; however, training in the performance of other

duties was also taken into account when information was available.)

(b) Nurturance training, i.e., training the child to be nurturant or helpful toward younger siblings and other dependent people.

(c) Obedience training.

(d) Self-reliance training.

(e) Achievement training, i.e., training the child to orient his behavior toward standards of excellence in performance, and to seek to achieve as excellent a performance as possible.

Where the term "no sex difference" is used here, it may mean any of three things: *(a)* the judge found separate evidence about the training of boys and girls on this particular variable, and judged it to be identical; *(b)* the judge found a difference between the training of boys and girls, but not great enough for the sexes to be rated a whole point apart on a seven-point scale; *(c)* the judge found evidence only about the training of "children" on this variable, the ethnographer not reporting separately about boys and girls.

SEX DIFFERENCES IN SOCIALIZATION

On the various aspects of attention and indulgence toward infants, the judges almost always agreed in finding no sex difference. Out of 96 cultures for which the ratings included the infancy period, 88 (92 per cent) were rated with no sex difference by either judge for any of those variables. This result is consistent with the point sometimes made by anthropologists that "baby" generally is a single status undifferentiated by sex, even though "boy" and "girl" are distinct statuses.

On the variables of childhood socialization, on the other hand, a rating of no sex difference by both judges was much less common. This finding of no sex difference varied in frequency from 10 per cent of the cultures for the achievement variable up to 62 per cent of the cultures for the obedience variable, as shown in the last column of Table 1. Where a sex difference is reported, by either one or both judges, the difference tends strongly to be in a particular direction, as shown in the earlier columns of the same table. Pressure toward nurturance, obedience, and responsibility

TABLE 1

RATINGS OF CULTURES FOR SEX DIFFERENCES ON FIVE VARIABLES
OF CHILDHOOD SOCIALIZATION PRESSURE

Variable	Number of cultures	Both judges agree in rating the variable higher in		One judge rates no difference, one rates the variable higher in		Percentage of cultures with evidence of sex differences in direction of		
		Girls	Boys	Girls	Boys	Girls	Boys	Neither
Nurturance	33	17	0	10	0	82%	0%	18%
Obedience	69	6	0	18	2	35%	3%	62%
Responsibility	84	25	2	26	7	61%	11%	28%
Achievement	31	0	17	1	10	3%	87%	10%
Self-reliance	82	0	64	0	6	0%	85%	15%

is most often stronger for girls, whereas pressure toward achievement and self-reliance is most often stronger for boys.

For nurturance and for self-reliance, all the sex differences
are in the same direction. For achievement there is only one
exception to the usual direction of difference, and for obedience
only two; but for responsibility there are nine. What do these
exceptions mean? We have reexamined all these cases. In most of
them, only one judge had rated the sexes as differently treated
(sometimes one judge, sometimes the other), and in the majority
of these cases both judges were now inclined to agree that there
was no convincing evidence of a real difference. There were
exceptions, however, especially in cases where a more formal or
systematic training of boys seemed to imply greater pressure on
them toward responsibility. The most convincing cases were the
Masai and Swazi, where both judges had originally agreed in
rating responsibility pressures greater in boys than in girls. In
comparing the five aspects of socialization we may conclude that
responsibility shows by far the strongest evidence of real variation in the direction of sex difference, and obedience much the
most frequently shows evidence of no sex difference at all.

In subsequent discussion we shall be assuming that the
obtained sex differences in the socialization ratings reflect true
sex differences in the cultural practices. We should consider here
two other possible sources of these rated differences.

1. The ethnographers could have been biased in favor of
seeing the same pattern of sex differences as in our culture.
However, most anthropologists readily perceive and eagerly
report novel and startling cultural features, so we may expect
them to have reported unusual sex differences where they
existed. The distinction between matrilineal and patrilineal, and
between matrilocal and patrilocal cultures, given prominence in
many ethnographic reports, shows an awareness of possible
variations in the significance of sex differences from culture to
culture.

2. The two judges could have expected to find in other
cultures the sex roles which are familiar in our culture and
inferred them from the material on the cultures. However, we
have reported only confident ratings, and such a bias seems less
likely here than for doubtful ratings. It might be argued, more-

over, that bias has more opportunity in the cases ambiguous enough so that only one judge reported a sex difference, and less opportunity in the cases where the evidence is so clear that both judges agree. Yet in general, as may be seen in Table 1, the deviant cases are somewhat more frequent among the cultures where only one judge reported a sex difference.

The observed differences in the socialization of boys and girls are consistent with certain universal tendencies in the differentiation of adult sex role. In the economic sphere, men are more frequently allotted tasks that involve leaving home and engaging in activities where a high level of skill yields important returns; hunting is a prime example. Emphasis on training in self-reliance and achievement for boys would function as preparation for such an economic role. Women, on the other hand, are more frequently allotted tasks at or near home that minister most immediately to the needs of others (such as cooking and water carrying); these activities have a nurturant character, and in their pursuit a responsible carrying out of established routines is likely to be more important than the development of an especially high order of skill. Thus training in nurturance, responsibility, and, less clearly, obedience, may contribute to preparation for this economic role. These consistencies with adult role go beyond the economic sphere, of course. Participation in warfare, as a male prerogative, calls for self-reliance and a high order of skill where survival or death is the immediate issue. The childbearing which is biologically assigned to women, and the child care which is socially assigned primarily to them, lead to nurturant behavior and often call for a more continuous responsibility than do the tasks carried out by men. Most of these distinctions in adult role are not inevitable, but the biological differences between the sexes strongly predispose the distinction of role, if made, to be in a uniform direction.[1]

The relevant biological sex differences are conspicuous in adulthood but generally not in childhood. If each generation were left entirely to its own devices, <u>therefore, without even an older</u> <u>generation to copy, sex differences in role would presumably be</u> <u>almost absent in childhood</u> and would have to be developed after

[1]For data and interpretations supporting various arguments of this paragraph, see Mead (2), Murdock (3), and Scheinfeld (6).

puberty at the expense of considerable relearning on the part of one or both sexes. Hence, a pattern of child training which foreshadows adult differences can serve the useful function of minimizing what Benedict termed "discontinuities in cultural conditioning"(1).

The differences in socialization between the sexes in our society, then, are no arbitrary custom of our society, but a very widespread adaptation of culture to the biological substratum of human life.

VARIATIONS IN DEGREE OF
SEX DIFFERENTIATION

While demonstrating near-universal tendencies in direction of difference between the socialization of boys and girls, our data do not show perfect uniformity. A study of the variations in our data may allow us to see some of the conditions which are associated with, and perhaps give rise to, a greater or smaller degree of this difference. For this purpose, we classified cultures as having relatively large or small sex difference by two different methods, one more inclusive and the other more selective. In both methods the ratings were at first considered separately for each of the five variables. A sex difference rating was made only if both judges made a rating on this variable and at least one judge's rating was confident.

In the more inclusive method the ratings were dichotomized, separately for each variable, as close as possible to the median into those showing a large and those showing a small sex difference. Thus, for each society a large or a small sex difference was recorded for each of the five variables on which a sex difference rating was available. A society was given an over-all classification of large or small sex difference if it had a sex difference rating on at least three variables and if a majority of these ratings agreed in being large, or agreed in being small. This method permitted classification of a large number of cultures, but the grounds for classification were capricious in many cases, as a difference of only one point in the rating of a single variable might change the over-all classification of sex difference for a culture from large to small.

In the more selective method, we again began by dichotomizing each variable as close as possible to the median; but a society was now classified as having a large or small sex difference on the variable only if it was at least one step away from the scores immediately adjacent to the median. Thus only the more decisive ratings of sex difference were used. A culture was classified as having an over-all large or small sex difference only if it was given a sex difference rating, which met this criterion on at least two variables, and only if all such ratings agreed in being large, or agreed in being small.

We then tested the relation of each of these dichotomies to 24 aspects of culture on which Murdock has categorized the customs of most of these societies[2] and which seemed of possible significance for sex differentiation. The aspects of culture covered include type of economy, residence pattern, marriage and incest rules, political integration, and social organization. For each aspect of culture, we grouped Murdock's categories to make a dichotomous contrast (sometimes omitting certain categories as irrelevant to the contrast). In the case of some aspects of culture, two or more separate contrasts were made (e.g., under form of marriage we contrasted monogamy with polygyny, and also contrasted sororal with nonsororal polygyny). For each of 40 comparisons thus formed, we prepared a 2×2 frequency table to determine relation to each of our sex-difference dichotomies. A significant relation was found for six of these 40 aspects of culture with the more selective dichotomization of over-all sex difference. In four of these comparisons, the relation to the more inclusive dichotomization was also significant. These relationships are all given in Table 2 (p. 106), in the form of phi coefficients, along with the outcome of testing significance by the use of χ^2 or Fisher's exact test. In trying to interpret these findings, we have also considered the nonsignificant correlations with other variables, looking for consistency and inconsistency with the general implications of the significant findings. We have arrived at the following formulation of results:

[2]These data were supplied to us directly by Professor Murdock.

1. Large sex difference in socialization is associated with an economy that places a high premium on the superior strength, and superior development of motor skills requiring strength, which characterize the male. Four of the correlations reported in Table 2 (p. 106) clearly point to this generalization: the correlations of large sex difference with the hunting of large animals, with grain rather than root crops, with the keeping of large rather than small domestic animals, and with nomadic rather than sedentary residence. The correlation with the unimportance of fishing may also be consistent with this generalization, but the argument is not clear.[3] Other correlations consistent with the generalization, though not statistically significant, are with large game hunting rather than gathering, with the hunting of large game rather than small game, and with the general importance of all hunting and gathering.

2. Large sex difference in socialization appears to be correlated with customs that make for a large family group with high cooperative interaction. The only statistically significant correlation relevant here is that with polygyny rather than monogamy. This generalization is, however, supported by several substantial correlations that fall only a little short of being statistically significant. One of these is a correlation with sororal rather than nonsororal polygyny; Murdock and Whiting (4) have presented indirect evidence that co-wives generally show smoother cooperative interaction if they are sisters. Correlations are also found with the presence of either an extended or a polygynous family

[3]Looking (with the more inclusive sample) into the possibility that this correlation might result from the correlation between fishing and sedentary residence, a complicated interaction between these variables was found. The correlation of sex differentiation with absence of fishing is found only in nomadic societies, where fishing is likely to involve cooperative activity of the two sexes, and its absence is likely to mean dependence upon the male for large game hunting or herding large animals (whereas in sedentary societies the alternatives to fishing do not so uniformly require special emphasis on male strength). The correlation of sex differentiation with nomadism is found only in nonfishing societies; here nomadism is likely to imply large game hunting or herding large animals, whereas in fishing societies nomadism evidently implies no such special dependence upon male strength. Maximum sex differentiation is found in nomadic nonfishing societies (15 with large difference and only 2 with small) and minimum sex differentiation in nomadic fishing societies (2 with large difference and 7 with small difference). These findings further strengthen the argument for a conspicuous influence of the economy upon sex differentiation.

rather than the nuclear family only; with the presence of an extended family; and with the extreme contrast between maximal extension and no extension of the family. The generalization is also to some extent supported by small correlations with wide extension of incest taboos, if we may presume that an incest taboo makes for effective unthreatening cooperation within the extended family. The only possible exception to this generalization, among substantial correlations, is a near-significant correlation with an extended or polygynous family's occupying a cluster of dwellings rather than a single dwelling.[4]

In seeking to understand this second generalization, we feel that the degree of social isolation of the nuclear family may perhaps be the crucial underlying variable. To the extent that the nuclear family must stand alone, the man must be prepared to take the woman's role when she is absent or incapacitated, and vice versa. Thus the sex differentiation cannot afford to be too great. But to the extent that the nuclear family is steadily interdependent with other nuclear families, the female role in the household economy can be temporarily taken over by another woman, or the male role by another man, so that sharp differentiation of sex role is no handicap.

The first generalization, which concerns the economy, cannot be viewed as dealing with material completely independent of the ratings of socialization. The training of children in their economic role was often an important part of the data used in rating socialization variables, and would naturally vary according to the general economy of the society. We would stress, however, that we were by no means using the identical data on the two sides of our comparison; we were on the one hand judging data on the socialization of children and on the other hand using

---

[4]We think the reverse of this correlation would be more consistent with our generalization here. But perhaps it may reasonably be argued that the various nuclear families composing an extended or polygynous family are less likely to develop antagonisms which hinder cooperation if they are able to maintain some physical separation. On the other hand, this variable may be more relevant to the first generalization than to the second. Occupation of a cluster of dwellings is highly correlated with presence of herding and with herding of large rather than small animals, and these economic variables in turn are correlated with large sex difference in socialization. Occupation of a cluster of dwellings is also correlated with polygyny rather than monogamy and shows no correlation with sororal vs. nonsororal polygyny.

Murdock's judgments on the economy of the adult culture. In the case of the second generalization, it seems to us that there was little opportunity for information on family and social structure to have influenced the judges in making the socialization ratings.

TABLE 2
CULTURE VARIABLES CORRELATED WITH LARGE
SEX DIFFERENCE IN SOCIALIZATION,
SEPARATELY FOR TWO TYPES
OF SAMPLE

Variable	*More selective sample*		*More inclusive sample*	
	ϕ	N	ϕ	N
Large animals are hunted	.48*	(34)	.28*	(72)
Grain rather than root crops are grown	.82**	(20)	.62**	(43)
Large or milking animals rather than small animals are kept	.65*	(19)	.43*	(35)
Fishing unimportant or absent	.42*	(31)	.19	(69)
Nomadic rather than sedentary residence	.61**	(34)	.15	(71)
Polygyny rather than monogamy	.51*	(28)	.38**	(64)

*$p < .05$.
**$p < .01$.
Note.—The variables have been so phrased that all correlations are positive. The phi coefficient is shown, and in parentheses, the number of cases on which the comparison was based. Significance level was determined by χ^2, or Fisher's exact test where applicable, using in all cases a two-tailed test.

Both of these generalizations contribute to understanding the social background of the relatively small difference in socialization of boys and girls which we believe characterizes our society at the present time. Our mechanized economy is perhaps less dependent than any previous economy upon the superior average strength of the male. The nuclear family in our society is often so isolated that husband and wife must each be prepared at times to take over or help in the household tasks normally assigned to the other. It is also significant that the conditions favoring low sex differentiation appear to be more characteristic of the upper segments of our society, in socioeconomic and educational status, than of lower segments. This observation may be relevant to the tendency toward smaller sex differences in personality in higher status groups (cf. Terman and Miles, 8).

The increase in our society of conditions favoring small sex difference has led some people to advocate a virtual elimination of sex differences in socialization. This course seems likely to be dysfunctional even in our society. Parsons, Bales, et al. (5) argue that a differentiation of role similar to the universal pattern of sex difference is an important and perhaps inevitable development in any social group, such as the nuclear family. If we add to their argument the point that biological differences between the sexes make most appropriate the usual division of those roles between the sexes, we have compelling reasons to expect that the decrease in differentiation of adult sex role will not continue to the vanishing point. In our training of children, there may now be less differentiation in sex role than characterizes adult life—so little, indeed, as to provide inadequate preparation for adulthood. This state of affairs is likely to be especially true of formal education, which is more subject to conscious influence by an ideology than is informal socialization at home. With child training being more oriented toward the male than the female role in adulthood, many of the adjustment problems of women in our society today may be partly traced to conflicts growing out of inadequate childhood preparation for their adult role. This argument is nicely supported in extreme form by Spiro's analysis of sex roles in an Israeli kibbutz (7). The ideology of the founders of the kibbutz included the objective of greatly reducing differences in sex role. But the economy of the kibbutz is a largely nonmechanized one in which the superior average strength of men is badly needed in many jobs. The result is that, despite the ideology and many attempts to implement it, women continue to be assigned primarily to traditional "women's work," and the incompatibility between upbringing or ideology and adult role is an important source of conflict for women.

Note on regional distribution. There is marked variation among regions of the world in typical size of sex difference in socialization. In our sample, societies in North America and Africa tend to have large sex difference, and societies in Oceania to have small sex difference. Less confidently, because of the smaller number of cases, we can report a tendency toward small sex differences in Asia and South America as well. Since most of the variables with which we find the sex difference to be significantly correlated have a similar regional distribution, the question arises whether the correlations might better be ascribed to some quite different source having to do with large regional similarities, rather than to the functional dependence we have suggested. As a partial check, we have tried to determine whether the correlations we report in Table 2 tend also to be found strictly within regions. For each of the three regions for which we have sizable samples (North America, Africa, and Oceania) we have separately plotted 2 × 2 tables corresponding to each of the 6 relationships reported in Table 2. (We did this only for the more inclusive sample, since for the more selective sample the number of cases within a region would have been extremely small.) Out of the 18 correlations thus determined, 11 are positive and only 3 are negative (the other 4 being exactly zero). This result clearly suggests a general tendency for these correlations to hold true within regions as well as between regions, and may lend further support to our functional interpretation.

Summary

A survey of certain aspects of socialization in 110 cultures shows that differentiation of the sexes is unimportant in infancy, but that in childhood there is, as in our society, a widespread pattern of greater pressure toward nurturance, obedience, and responsibility in girls, and toward self-reliance and achievement striving in boys. There are a few reversals of sex difference, and many instances of no detectable sex difference; these facts tend to confirm the cultural rather than directly biological nature of the differences. Cultures vary in the degree to which these differentiations are made; correlational analysis suggests some of the social conditions influencing these variations, and helps in understanding why our society has relatively small sex differentiation.

REFERENCES

1. Benedict, Ruth. 1938. Continuities and discontinuities in cultural conditioning. *Psychiatry* 1: 161–67.
2. Mead, Margaret. 1949. *Male and female.* New York: Morrow.
3. Murdock, G. P. 1937. Comparative data on the division of labor by sex. *Social Forces* 15: 551–53.
4. Murdock, G. P., and J. W. M. Whiting. 1951. Cultural determination of parental attitudes: The relationship between the social structure, particularly family structure and parental behavior. In M. J. E. Senn (ed.), *Problems of infancy and childhood: Transactions of the Fourth Conference,* March 6–7, 1950. New York: Josiah Macy, Jr. Foundation. Pp. 13–34.
5. Parsons, T.; R. F. Bales; et al. 1955. *Family, socialization and interaction process.* Glencoe, Ill.: Free Press.
6. Scheinfeld, A. 1944. *Women and men.* New York: Harcourt, Brace.
7. Spiro, M. E. 1956. *Kibbutz: Venture in utopia.* Cambridge, Mass.: Harvard University Press.
8. Terman, L. M., and Catherine C. Miles. 1936. *Sex and personality.* New York: McGraw-Hill.

8

Entrepreneurial Environments and the Emergence of Achievement Motivation in Adolescent Males

JONATHAN H. TURNER

INTRODUCTION

The relevance of achievement motivation to social structural processes has been well documented over the last decade. Need for achievement, or the desire to excel in accordance with standards of excellence (McClelland et al., 1953), has been found to be intimately connected with economic development (McClelland, 1961; Rosen, 1964), social and ethnic stratification (Rosen, 1956, 1959), educational achievement (Elder, 1965; Rosen, 1958), occupational aspirations (Elder, 1962, 1968), mobility (Crockett, 1962), and other social processes. Concomitant to studies documenting the centrality of achievement motivation to these processes have been attempts to discern the origins of such motivation. The predominant emphasis in this search has been on family

Jonathan H. Turner, "Entrepreneurial Environments and the Emergence of Achievement Motivation in Adolescent Males," *Sociometry* 33 (June 1970): 147–65.

interaction between parents and sons. In Winterbottom's (1958) pioneering study, two types of parental training practices, independence-mastery and achievement, were found to be associated with high need-achievement in male subjects. Rosen and D'Andrade (1959) similarly documented the operation of these training practices, while discovering that a particular pattern in the division of labor between parents was also crucial. Their data suggest that high need-achievers come from families where both parents emphasize achievement, but where independence-mastery training comes from the father and achievement training, accomplished by high nurturance, from the mother. Other data (Rosen, 1961, 1962) indicate that there are certain optimal ages at which implementation of these training practices leads to high levels of achievement motivation, although these optimal ages vary from one culture to another (McClelland, 1961).

As has now been demonstrated, there are also class differences with respect to such socialization practices (Hammond, 1954; Komarvosky, 1962, pp. 76–86; McKinely, 1964; Kohn, 1959). Middle and upper middle class parents apparently are the most likely to engage in those socialization practices critical in the emergence of need-achievement; and it is from these classes that high need-achievement among adolescent males has been consistently reported (Rosen, 1956, 1964).

Thus, the origins of need-achievement have been traced to two related social structures, family and social class. Evidently, there is "something" about the middle classes which affects family socialization in those ways conducive to high need-achievement. It is this "something" which will be examined in this paper.

OCCUPATION AS A VARIABLE

Several studies offer a clue as to what it is about processes in the middle classes which results in high achievement motivation. Pearlin and Kohn (1963) found that the nature of a father's occupation was critical in determining parental orientations toward socialization. The more a father worked with people and the less with things, and the less he was supervised by others and the more autonomy he had at work, the more he and his wife would stress achievement, independence, and self-reliance to their children. Although their findings were more ambiguous, Miller and Swanson (1958) discovered that in families where the father's occupation required high self-reliance, autonomy, and decision-making, there was a somewhat greater emphasis on child rearing practices which emphasized self-control and self-reliance (i.e., independence and mastery) than in families where the father's occupation did not require such behavior.

These data suggest that it is the nature of father's occupation, rather than the more encompassing variable of social class which is the significant force in altering family socialization in a direction conducive to high need-achievement. However, there are few conclusive data demonstrating that this is the case (McClelland, 1961). To the extent that this can be demonstrated, more specific understanding of the social structural origins of this motivational state will be possible. Therefore, the specific research question concerning the present study is: in what ways does father's occupation, *per se,* affect the level of need-achievement among adolescent males?

Procedures

It was decided that a broad range of occupational types would be desirable in order to examine adequately the influence of this variable on achievement motivation. Later these occupations would be grouped for analysis, but initially a wide range of occupations was sought.

Area of Study. To secure this diversity, occupations in a number of vastly different communities located in different areas of a Southern state were studied. These communities, and the occupational structure therein, are briefly summarized below:

The Transitional

This community was in a period of rapid industrialization. Only fifteen years ago, the majority of household heads were low income, subsistence farmers who used horse-drawn plows to cultivate small tracts (around forty acres) of land. In recent years, three factories from outside the community have located close to the community and have drawn all but 16 per cent of family heads off the farm. A small central business district has emerged, but little urbanism exists, because families continue to live on their now unattended farms with fathers commuting short distances to work. A few white collar (7 per cent) jobs in the factories and in the business district exist, but the clear majority of the working population (62 per cent) are routine blue collar workers in factories and in non-industrial jobs. Some blue collar workers hold high level supervisory positions in industry or own their own businesses (e.g., gas station, garage, store, etc.) in the community (15 per cent).

The Industrial

This community, located next to a large urban city in an adjacent state, had been industrial for over one hundred years. Three cotton mills, recently converted to synthetic production, have existed since the Civil War and provided employment for the majority of household heads. A few white collar occupations are evident (7 per cent) and some blue collar workers own their own businesses or hold supervisory positions in the mills. But the mills and a few non-industrial occupations provide routine, semi-skilled, manual work for 75 per cent of the male family heads in the community. The community is highly urbanized with small frame houses clustered around the mills and a small business district. The industrial community can thus be considered a typical working class community.

The Modern

This community was a middle to upper-middle class suburb of the most modern city of the state. Over 85 per cent of the working fathers in this suburb were employed in white collar occupations with nearly 70 per cent of these employed in large bureaucracies. 17 per cent of these white collar workers owned their own business. 14 per cent of the fathers in the community were employed in highly paid manual occupations (over $9,000 per year). The community can thus be considered a typical suburban, middle class area of a large urban center.

The fact that these three communities are Southern might appear to limit the generalizability of findings. Yet, this is probably a legitimate indictment of any study conducted in only one region of the country. Even if the Southern communities are less typical than communities in other regions (and this might be the case), the focus of this study is on the occupational types within these communities, not the communities themselves. The communities were selected because they were dominated by certain key occupations necessary to investigate the research problem of this study. And these occupations cannot be considered unique to the South. Furthermore, as will be indicated in the hypothesis, we are interested in establishing the influence of occupation, *per se,* on a child's level of need-achievement, regardless of community influences. Utilizing Southern communities which might be considered more homogeneous, cohesive, and constraining than communities in other regions is perhaps the best way to establish the independent influence of father's occupation on son's level of achievement motivation.

Sampling.   In each community, the entire seventh and eighth grade male population present at school on a given day was studied. Absenteeism in all cases was under five per cent.

Tests.   (a) Subjects were given an extensive questionnaire on their father's occupation. This questionnaire utilized a large and varied battery of questions.[1] Information gathered from this

[1]The questionnaire included forced choice, Likert-type, fill-in-the-blank, and essay questions. Some examples of each type of question are reported below: *fill-in-the-blank:* What is the name of the place where your father works?; What is your father's job title there—what is he called?; *forced choice:* How many people work where your father works?; Is it a big company—how big?; How much money per year does your father make at his job?; Does your father have a boss?; How many bosses does your father have?; Does your father own his own business?; Does your father work for a company or business owned by others? If so, what kind?; Does your father supervise others at work? If so, how many would you guess?; *Likert-type:* How much is your father required to do things on his own at work, without supervision?; How free from supervision at work is your father?; *essay:* Describe what your father does on a typical day at work; Tell us as much as you know about your father's work.

source became the basis for classifying the occupation of a subject's father. There are a number of deficiencies in collecting father's occupational data in this way: (1) Adolescents may possess little knowledge about their father's occupation. However, in their answers to the questionnaire administered in this study, son's reports on their father's occupation were detailed and comprehensive. (2) Yet, while adolescents may appear informed and articulate about their father's occupation, they may be *mis*informed and thus articulate highly distorted reports. (3) And more seriously, distortion in these reports could be related to a child's need for achievement. That is, adolescent perceptions and descriptions of father's occupation may be a function of their own level of achievement motivation. Should this be the case, separating the two major variables of this study—father's occupation and son's need for achievement—would be impossible. The former would be a reflection and extension of the latter. While these three methodological deficiencies could distort findings, such did not appear to be the case. Although very brief, school records never failed to confirm a subject's description of his father's occupation. Also, an analysis of high and low need-achievers' essays did not reveal differences in style or exuberance. This would be expected if high need-achievers were distorting their essays in accordance with their own achievement fantasies.

(b) Subjects were also administered the Thematic Apperception Tests developed by McClelland and his associates to measure achievement motivation (McClelland et al., 1953).

Scoring of Tests.   (a) The TAT essays were scored in strict accordance with the procedures outlined by McClelland and his collaborators (Atkinson, 1958).

(b) The occupational questionnaire was designed to reveal a father's occupational status and his role behavior in that status. The questionnaire focused primarily on whether or not a father engaged in what was called *entrepreneurial* role behavior in his occupation status. Following McClelland (1961), the analytical elements of entrepreneurial role behavior were isolated. In order for role behavior to be considered *entrepreneurial,* it had to involve at least these four elements: (1) a high degree of autonomy or freedom from direct supervision by others; (2) authority over at least two levels of subordinates; (3) decision-making obligations; and (4) coordinating resources, men and/or materials. Other schemes (McClelland, 1961) include additional elements as components of entrepreneurship: "risk taking," "instrumental focus" and extensive "reliance on feedback." These can rightfully be considered as crucial elements of entrepreneurial role behavior; but if an actor has autonomy, and must supervise others, coordinate resources, and make decisions, it can be inferred that he is also engaging in these other behaviors. However, this conceptualization of entrepreneurship does not follow Schumpeter (1934) in explicitly considering the "innovative" component of entrepreneurship, nor Miller and Swanson (1958) in distinguishing "entrepreneurs" from "welfare bureaucrats." The innovative component of entrepreneurship is not included in the present conceptualization because it is difficult to measure. Omission of Miller and Swanson's (1958) distinction is more substantive. It is felt that they set up a false dichotomy by viewing entrepreneurs displaying such traits as rationality, instrumentality, self-control, independence, and manipulativeness as existing primarily outside large scale bureaucracies. This certainly is not the case, for high level managers in most modern bureaucracies must also display these traits in order to fulfill their organizational obligations. The same is true of many high level foremen in blue collar occupations. Entrepreneurial role behavior can thus occur in a wide variety of structures—bureaucratic or otherwise—in modern societies. One of the mistaken assumptions in much of the literature (Miller & Swanson, 1958; Riesman, 1950; Mills, 1956) is that entrepreneurship is a vanishing role; whereas in reality, only its structural locus has changed from the small, independent business to the large scale organization. For this reason, it is considered more prudent to define analytically entrepreneurial roles regardless of their structural locus.

By applying the four criteria listed above to the subjects' reports on their fathers' occupational status, it was possible in most cases to determine whether or not a father engaged in entrepreneurial role behavior. If he did, his occupation was considered *entrepreneurial*. Within this *entrepreneurial* category, several types of occupational status-roles were considered to be important for subsequent purposes of comparison:

    (1) White Collar Status-roles
        A. Managers in bureaucracies
        B. Owners of a business
    (2) Blue Collar Status-roles
        A. Managers in an industry or factory
        B. Owners of a business
    (3) Farmers
        A. Manager of a farm
        B. Owner of a farm

White Collar Managers were white collar entrepreneurs who worked for a wage in a large organization (at least one hundred employees) where they had autonomy and where they supervised at least two levels of subordinates, comprising no less than fifty employees. The same criteria were applied to *Blue Collar Managers,* except that they worked in a production-based, rather than service-based, organization. *Owners of a Business,* whether blue or white collar, were those who owned and actively ran a business and had at least six subordinates. An entrepreneurial *Owner of a Farm* was a father who worked on a farm of more than two hundred acres which yielded an income of at least $5,000 per year. *A Manager of a Farm* was a father who supervised at least two levels of subordinates on a farm exceeding one thousand acres. These occupational types were established prior to the collection of the data.

Different types of entrepreneurial status-roles were distinguished because it was felt important to separate middle class entrepreneurs from working class entrepreneurs. Manual entrepreneurial status-roles in factories (or farms) cannot be considered middle class in terms of income, prestige and esteem, or requisite level of education. On the other hand, most white collar entrepreneurial status-roles can be considered "middle class" with respect to these variables. Entrepreneurship, as it has been defined in this paper, can occur across various social classes and thus it was necessary to distinguish intrepreneurship from social class. Only in this way could the research question of this study be examined: in what what ways does father's occupation, *per se,* lead to high achievement motivation among adolescent males?

With respect to *non-entrepreneurial* occupations, the following types of status-roles were established prior to data collection: (1) Routine White Collar, (2) Routine Blue Collar, and (3) Subsistence Farm.

A *Routine White Collar* employee was a father who worked for a wage, worked for others, or in an organization, in a non-manual capacity, and had little authority or autonomy. A *Routine Blue Collar* status-role was one in which an employee worked with his hands, worked for a wage, worked for others or in an organization, and had minimal authority or autonomy. *Subsistence Farmers* were fathers who owned, rented, or share-cropped a small tract of land which yielded only a subsistence living. These distinctions among *non-entrepreneurial* status-roles were made for the same reason as the distinctions with respect to *entrepreneurial* occupations: many non-entrepreneurial status-roles are middle class (e.g., most white collar occupations), whereas most blue collar and farm subsistence occupations cannot be considered middle class; and if occupation, *per se,* was to be examined, it had to be separated from social class which encompasses many other variables (e.g., neighborhood, life style, prestige, income, education, etc.).

Except for 13 per cent of the subjects, fathers in each community could be placed into one of the broad categories described above. Approximately 10 per cent of the fathers could not be classified because the data supplied by their sons were incomplete and/or ambiguous. Another 3 per cent of the subjects were from homes in which a father no longer resided and data on these subjects were not analyzed.

HYPOTHESIS

With these procedures, data on father's occupation and son's level of achievement motivation could be gathered in three entirely different types of communities (the transitional, the industrial, and the modern). In turn this would enable data on different types of occupations to be collected (white collar, blue collar, and farm; entrepreneurial and non-entrepreneurial). Furthermore, since the modern community was almost completely middle class and the industrial and transitional almost completely working class, it was considered possible to compare data on adolescents' need for achievement from different social classes.

Before the data were gathered, this hypothesis was formulated:

Regardless of community structure, social class, or type of occupation, sons of fathers in entrepeneurial *occupations would display significantly higher levels of achievement motivation than sons of fathers in* non-entrepreneurial *occupations.*

RESULTS

In Table 1, the mean achievement motivation scores of sons of entrapreneurial and non-entrepreneurial fathers are reported for each community.[2] The over-all achievement motivation score for the total sample is also reported. The mean differences in achievement motivation scores between sons of entrepreneurs and non-entrepreneurs within each community are statistically significant (one-tailed *t* test) at better than the .001 level, as is the over-all difference. In regard to the hypothesis of this study, the large over-all difference in achievement motivation between sons of entrepreneurs and non-entrepreneurs strongly supports the hypothesis. The comparatively small differences between achievement scores across communities suggest that while community may have some influence on an adolescent's level of achievement motivation, the nature of a father's occupation, whether entrepreneurial or non-entrepreneurial, has considerably more influence.[3]

[2]With McClelland's scoring procedures, a range of TAT scores -4 to $+11$ is possible for each subject. Since the computer cannot handle conveniently minus scores, a constant of $+5$ was added to each score, making the possible range for each subject $+1$ to $+16$.

[3]While two-way analysis of variance would have allowed meaningful comparisons of data within and across communities, the *N*s are not sufficiently similar to warrant the use of this technique. Also, since the mean differences are so large within communities, and considerably smaller across communities, a significance test of this sort is less crucial.

TABLE 1
$\bar{x}$ TAT SCORES OF SONS FROM ENTREPRENEURIAL AND NON-ENTREPRENEURIAL
ENVIRONMENTS FOR EACH COMMUNITY

Community	Achievement scores*		N^{**}
	Sons of entrepreneurs	Sons of non-entrepreneurs	
The transitional	9.7(41)	3.7(146)	187
The industrial	9.0(41)	3.4(124)	165
The modern	9.6(111)	4.8(176)	289
Over-all	9.5(193)	4.1(446)	Total: 639

* All *within* community differences significant at better than the .001 level. The transitional: $t = 8.6$, $df = 48.1$; The industrial: $t = 6.3$, $df = 41.2$; The modern: $t = 6.1$, $df = 37.1$; The over-all χ differences: $t = 13.2$, $df = 22.5$, $p < .001$.

** Because the Ns and Standard Deviations in the various subsamples in this and following tables are quite different, a correction for this is made to better approximate the correct degrees of freedom in each t test. The procedures used in this and the following tables are outlined in Blalock (1960:175–76) when Ns and Standard Deviations in samples are unequal.

In Table 2, the mean achievement motivation scores of subjects from entrepreneurial and non-entrepreneurial environments are reported with respect to social class. Because of incomplete data, only a crude classification of sons into "middle" and "working" classes was possible.[4] However, since previous studies have demonstrated this class line to be the most significant in terms of differences in need-achievement (Rosen, 1956, 1964), this classification of subjects into "middle" and "working" classes should allow examination of social class influences on achievement motivation. The differences in achievement motivation reported in Table 2 between sons of entrepreneurs and non-entrepreneurs within either the working or middle class are statistically significant at better than the .001 level (one-tailed t test). Sons of both working class and middle class entrepreneurs display significantly higher levels of need-achievement than their counterparts from non-entrepreneurial environments. As could be expected from previous studies (Rosen, 1956, 1964), the over-all class difference is statistically significant at the .001 level. The class difference in the achievement scores of sons from non-entrepreneurial environments is also statistically significant. This could either reflect a social class or community difference. Since most of the middle class non-entrepreneurs are from the modern community and most of the working class non-entrepreneurs (but not all) are from the transitional and industrial communities, it is difficult to determine which variable—social class or community—is causing this statistically significant difference. However, the class differences with respect to sons of entrepreneurs are *not* statistically significant. Since most of the working class entrepreneurs come from the transitional and industrial communities and a majority of the middle class entrepreneurs from the modern community, it is clear with respect to sons of entrepreneurs that social class, even when com-

[4]The social class of a subject was established by two criteria: (1) type of job, whether white collar or blue collar; and (2) level of father's yearly income. A middle class subject was one whose father was white collar and earned over $7,000 per year, while a "working class" subject was one whose father worked in a blue collar job, regardless of income. Naturally, this classification ignores such important class variables as level of education prestige, neighborhood, life style, family background, etc., but the data were inadequate for a more extensive classification.

TABLE 2

x̄ TAT SCORES OF SONS FROM ENTREPRENEURIAL AND NON-ENTREPRENEURIAL
ENVIRONMENTS BY SOCIAL CLASS

Social class	Achievement scores		
	Sons of entrepreneurs	Sons of non-entrepreneurs	Over-all
Working Class	8.8(57)	3.6(308)	4.6(365)
	*	**	***
	+		
Middle Class	9.7(136)	4.7(138)	7.1(274)
		++	
			Total N:639

*t = 1.03, df = 51.3, N.S.
***t = 3.52, df = 47.1, p < .001
***t = 6.9, df = 56.6, p < .001
+t = 6.6, df = 36.3, p < .001
++t = 10.2, df = 46.2, p < .001

pounded by community differences, has little, if any, influence on achievement motivation. Thus, the over-all difference in need-achievement means between social classes is explained not so much in terms of social class, but in terms of the differential distribution of entrepreneurial occupations in the middle classes (49 per cent as opposed to 15 per cent in the working class). With respect to the hypothesis of this study, these findings indicate that while social class apparently has some impact on the level of achievement motivation of adolescents, the nature of a father's occupation has considerably more. Class differences in achievement motivation thus do not "explain away" the differences in achievement motivation predicted in the hypothesis and originally reported in Table 1.

In Table 3, the achievement scores of adolescents from different types of occupational environments in the modern community are reported. The levels of achievement motivation of sons whose fathers are in *Routine White Collar, Routine Blue Collar, White Collar Manager,* and *White Collar Owner* (of a business) status-roles are compared. As is clear, the achievement scores of adolescents whose fathers are in *Routine White Collar* and *Blue Collar* status-roles converge, as do those of sons of *White Collar Managers* and *Owners* (of a business). As would be expected on the basis of the data in Tables 1 and 2, the largest differences in achievement motivation within the community are between sons from *entrepreneurial* and *non-entrepreneurial* environments. Differences between occupational types within either the entrepreneurial or non-entrepreneurial categories are not statistically significant. Also of interest is the fact that with the possible exception of sons whose fathers are *Routine Blue Collar* workers most occupations within this community can be considered middle class. Since many sons of these middle class fathers do not possess high need for achievement (i.e., sons of *Routine White Collar* workers), it can be tentatively concluded that variations in occupational environments *within* the middle classes lead to wide variations in a son's level of achievement motivation. This indicates that it is not social class, *per se,* which generates high achievement motivation, but particular types of occupations within these classes. The fact that entrepreneurial occupations are more likely to exist in the middle class might well account for the high level of achievement motivation of adolescents from the middle classes consistently reported in earlier studies (Rosen, 1956, 1964). The data in Table 3 also help explain and specify the results reported in Table 2 above where achievement scores of subjects varied less with respect to social class than with occupation.

TABLE 3
$\bar{X}$ TAT SCORES OF SONS FROM DIFFERENT ECONOMIC
ENVIRONMENTS WITHIN THE MODERN COMMUNITY

Father's occupation	*Achievement scores of sons +*
Routine Blue Collar Worker	4.6(38)
*	
Routine White Collar Worker	4.8(138)
Entrepreneurial White Collar Managers	9.3(61)
*	
Entrepreneurial White Collar Owners	10.1(50)
Total *N:* 287	

+Differences between all occupational types significant at .001 level: $F = 38.9$ (one-way), $p < .001$.
*Not significant (two tailed *t* test)

Of particular theoretical interest in this table is the finding that entrepreneurs in bureaucratic organizations and owners of a business in the modern community *both* seem to generate high achievement motivation in their sons. With respect to the extensive literature (Riesman, 1951; Mills, 1951; Miller & Swanson, 1958; Presthus, 1962) hypothesizing the negative impact of modern bureaucratic organizations on such character traits as "inner directedness," "achievement," "ambition," and the like, the findings of this study are relevant. Perhaps they give some indication of the conditions under which this hypothesis holds. The data clearly indicate that owners of a business or Mills' "independent entrepreneur" or Miller and Swanson's (1958) "entrepreneur" and Riesman's (1951) "inner directed man" affect their sons' level of achievement motivation in ways that a routine bureaucrat does not. But, as noted earlier, these authors seem to have underemphasized the many entrepreneurial status positions within bureaucracies which appear to require the same type of role behavior as the "independent entrepreneur." This is supported by the findings in Table 3 that these bureaucratic managerial entrepreneurs seem to affect their sons' level of achievement motivation in the same way as the independent entrepreneur. Naturally, it is ucertain as to whether or not achievement motivation as measured in this study is the same thing as Riesman, Mills, Presthus et al., are talking about; but to the extent that it is, their pessimistic conclusions about a bureaucratized social structure seem unwarranted.

In Table 4, the mean level of achievement motivation of sons from various occupational environments is reported for the industrial community. Because of the small *N, Blue Collar* and *White Collar* entrepreneurial occupations could not be subdivided into *Manager* and *Owner* (of a business) types. As indicated above, the occupational types and categories were established prior to data collection and thus it could be expected that insufficient cases would cause the elimination of some categories. Nevertheless, the data can be analyzed with respect to the hypothesis of this study. Sons of entrepreneurs, whether white or blue collar, have much higher achievement scores than sons of non-entrepreneurs. This is consistent with findings reported in Tables 1 and 2. It can also be noted that since sons of *Routine Blue Collar* workers in this community have lower mean achievement scores than their counterparts in the modern community, other influences besides father's occupation are apparently operative. Here again, perhaps other variables associated with social class or community raise somewhat the level of need achievement among sons of *Routine Blue Collar* workers in the modern community. Because of the small *N* in the *White Collar* entrepreneur category, no conclusions can be drawn about the differences

TABLE 4
$\bar{\chi}$ TAT SCORES OF SONS IN DIFFERENT ECONOMIC
ENVIRONMENTS IN THE INDUSTRIAL COMMUNITY

Father's occupation	Achievement scores of sons +
Routine Blue Collar	3.4(124)
Entrepreneurial Blue Collar	7.5(30)
Entrepreneurial White Collar*	12.4(11)
Total *N:*	165

*There were no Routine White Collar Occupations in this community.
+Over-all mean differences significant at the .001 level: $F = 38.8$ (one-way), $p < .001$.

in achievement scores of sons from this and *Blue Collar* entrepreneur category.

In Table 5, the mean achievement motivation scores of sons from different occupational environments are reported for the transitional community. As in Table 4, the *Blue Collar* and *White Collar* entrepreneurial categories are collapsed because of insufficient cases. Also, to the investigator's surprise, all subjects from farm environments came from *Farm Subsistence* occupational backgrounds and thus the *Farm Owner* and *Farm Manager* occupational categories proved irrelevant.[5] The data do reveal, however, the same pattern as in Table 4: sons of *White Collar* and *Blue Collar* entrepreneurs have higher levels of achievement motivation than sons whose fathers are either *Routine Blue Collar* workers or *Subsistence Farmers.* Again, the Ns are too small to warrant any firm statements about the mean differences (which are great) between *Blue Collar* and *White Collar* entrepreneurs.

TABLE 5
$\bar{X}$ TAT SCORES OF SONS FROM DIFFERENT ECONOMIC ENVIRONMENTS IN THE TRANSITIONAL COMMUNITY

Father's occupation	Achievement score of sons*
Subsistence Farmer	3.0(30)
**	
Routine Blue Collar Worker	3.9(116)
Entrepreneurial Blue Collar Worker	10.3(27)
Entrepreneurial White Collar Worker+	7.9(14)
	Total N: 187

*Over-all differences among all occupations significant at the .001 level: $F = 30.5$, $P < .001$.

**Not Significant (one tailed t test)

+There were only two white collar routine workers in the community and therefore, the data on them are not reported here or in the other tables.

[5]Thus, in terms of filling all the occupational categories established prior to data collection, the data did not completely accommodate the research design. Nevertheless, meaningful comparisons between a sufficient number of occupational categories was possible so that the research question of this study could be seriously examined and conclusions drawn (see below).

Discussion

Sons of entrepreneurs in three vastly different types of community structure and from different social classes consistently display a high level of achievement motivation. Sons of non-entrepreneurs, irrespective of community or social class, reveal low levels of achievement motivation. Findings thus lend strong support to the hypothesis of this study.

Previous research has indicated that adolescents with high need-achievement are over-represented in the middle classes (Rosen, 1956, 1964). Other research has revealed that particular kinds of family socialization practices are conducive to high achievement motivation (Winterbottom, 1958; Rosen & D'Andrade, 1959; Strodbeck, 1958). The findings of this study begin to point to *what it is* about social class which affects family socialization in ways conducive to high need for achievement (Table 1). While social class variables besides father's occupation probably have some impact on need-achievement, the nature of a father's occupation apparently has more influence (Table 2). Previous research demonstrating high need-achievement to be disproportionately represented in the middle classes can now, to some extent, be accounted for by the disproportionate number of enterpreneurial occupations in these classes. Conversely, the low level of need-achievement typical of working class adolescents is probably due to the comparative lack of such entrepreneurial occupations in this class. However, some blue collar occupations are entrepreneurial; and to the extent that they are, sons of these working class entrepreneurs will display levels of achievement motivation roughly equivalent to their middle class counterparts (Table 2). The fact that this relationship stands up within three entirely different types of communities further supports this conclusion (Tables 3, 4, and 5).

However, the data cannot indicate through what specific causal sequence a father's occupational experience is affecting his son's level of achievement motivation. Although it appears reasonable to conclude that a father's occupation affects family socialization which in turn influences son's level of achievement motivation, this cannot be demonstrated, since no data on the socialization experiences of subjects was collected. But in light of the existing literature on family socialization and the emergence of achievement motivation (Winterbottom, 1958; Rosen, 1961; Rosen & D'Andrade, 1959) as well as the literature on occupational participation and family socialization (Aberle & Naegele, 1952; McKinely, 1964; Miller & Swanson, 1958; Pearlin & Kohn, 1966), it can be argued that this is the most probable sequence of causation. Although the exact processes in this causal nexus are not clearly understood, two dominant hypotheses are revealed in the literature:

(1) Occupational Values and Family Socialization

Several studies suggest that various occupational experiences of father result in an ideology or set of values which lead to an emphasis on particular kinds of socialization practices by parents (Aberle & Naegele, 1952; Elder, 1965; Kohn, 1959; Pearlin & Kohn, 1966). Results of these studies indicate that occupations requiring responsibility, decision-making, competition, and aggressiveness result in an occupational ideology stressing achievement. Subsequently, this ideology is absorbed by the wife with the result that emphasis on achievement by both parents becomes a predominant training practice, especially with regard to sons.

(2) Occupational Frustration-Aggression and Family Socialization

Other studies demonstrate that some occupations induce greater frustrations than others and that the more frustrating the job is for a father, the more aggressive and dominant toward spouse and children he becomes (McKinely, 1964; Hammond, 1954). A father who is closely supervised, and who has little autonomy, decision-making power, or authority accumulates frustrations leading to the expression of aggressions in the family which cannot be expressed in the workplace. This apparently results in severe sanctioning of children. Conversely, a father who can exercise authority and who has autonomy and freedom on the job will be less frustrated and thus more likely to be nurturant and emphasize independence and mastery to his son.

Taken together, these two hypotheses offer at least a partial explanation for the findings in this paper. Occupational experience seemingly affects fathers on both an ideological and psychological level. Achievement values and ideology, acquired more readily in entrepreneurial status-roles, become absorbed by the wife with the result that both parents engage in achievement training, a crucial condition for the emergence of achievement motivation in sons (Rosen & D'Andrade, 1959). But as Strodbeck (1958) notes, achievement training is not necessarily accompanied by independence and mastery training, since many parents tend to over-emphasize achievement to such an extent that they dominate their sons. And to the degree that an achievement ideology acquired in the workplace hinders independence-mastery training, achievement motivation in sons will be correspondingly low. Thus, an achievement ideology acquired in an entrepreneurial status-role is a necessary, but not sufficient, condition for the emergence of achievement motivation. Perhaps the sufficient condition then becomes the psychological experience of fathers in their jobs. Because entrepreneurs have autonomy and decision-making powers, they are less likely than non-entrepreneurs to accumulate those frustrations at work which become displaced into aggressiveness, and hence parental dominance, in the family. In turn, this could increase the probability that entrepreneurs would be more nurturant and more apt to emphasize independence-mastery to their sons, the other critical condition for achievement motivation (Rosen & D'Andrade, 1959).

Therefore, to the extent that an occupation promotes achievement values in a father, while allowing few intense frustrations to develop, it may affect family structure and socialization in those ways conducive to achievement motivation in sons. In modern social systems, entrepreneurial occupations are the most likely to meet these two conditions. However, since no data on father's level of need-achievement or his socialization experiences were collected, this causal sequence can be seriously questioned. Perhaps fathers in entrepreneurial occupations fill such positions by virtue of a high level of need-achievement which they had before entering the entrepreneurial status role. High need-achievement made such an occupation attractive to

these fathers, while giving them the psychological quality necessary for successful role performance. It could then be concluded
that it is father's need-achievement, *per se,* and not his occupational experience which accounts for the clear relationship reported above.[6] Results reported by McClelland (1961) clearly
demonstrate that at least middle class entrepreneurs (what we
have called *managers*) in several countries, including the United
States, do possess a significantly higher level of need-
achievement than a control group of equally educated non-
managers. But as to whether high need-achievement emerged
before or after involvement in an entrepreneurial status role is
not determined.

A study utilizing at least three matched (age, education,
income, etc.) samples would be necessary in order to resolve this
"chicken and egg" dilemma: (1) One sample would be composed
of fathers who had been entrepreneurs for an extended period of
time, and their sons; (2) another sample would be composed of
fathers who have just become entrepreneurs, and their sons; (3) a
sample of fathers who had never been, nor were likely to be,
entrepreneurs, and their sons, would also be necessary. All
fathers and sons would then be given need-achievement tests
(with perhaps, fathers also being given a value orientation
questionnaire). With these procedures, the effects on son's need
for achievement of father's achievement motivation in a variety
of occupational status-roles could be examined. However, if the
sons of fathers with high need-achievement in both entrepreneurial and non-entrepreneurial occupations turned out to
have the same level of need-achievement, then the issue would
not be resolved, since there is a confounding variable in such a
finding: anticipatory socialization. It is likely that occupation is
still exerting an influence, because non-entrepreneurs with high
achievement motivation probably desire and anticipate becoming
managers. And thus, they have probably undergone anticipatory
socialization into the entrepreneurial perspective. In turn, these

---

[6]This is also the problem encountered by studies reported above dealing
with the relationship between father's occupation and certain socialization
practices: fathers in particular occupations may have had those characteristics
deemed critical to the emergence of a set of socialization practices prior to
incumbency in a particular kind of occupational status-role.

fathers might socialize their sons in ways very similar to those of established entrepreneurs. This kind of finding, which is likely in any study collecting data at only one point in time, points to the ultimate need for a longitudinal design. Only with the latter can changes in father's need-achievement and occupational status-role as they affect sons' need for achievement be recorded.

SUMMARY

Existing research has suggested that certain occupational experiences of fathers affect family socialization in ways which might, in light of other literature, be conducive to high need-achievement among adolescent males. Although no studies of achievement motivation have explicitly demonstrated this to be the case, the well documented findings on family socialization and the emergence of achievement motivation seem to "fit" nicely with findings on occupational experiences of fathers and family socialization practices. Drawing from these two bodies of literature, fathers in particular kinds of occupations—namely, the entrepreneurial—were hypothesized to have sons with higher levels of achievement motivation than sons of fathers in non-entrepreneurial occupations. In different community types, social classes, and occupations this hypothesis was strongly supported by the data. Although the data do not permit examination of the causal sequence through which a father's occupational experience affects his sons' level of achievement motivation, two compatible hypotheses are offered to explain the findings of this study. Fathers in entrepreneurial occupations are seen as having a set of values and psychological dispositions compatible with those socialization practices in the family which will lead to high need for achievement in their sons.

REFERENCES

Aberle, F., and K. Naegele. 1952. Middle class father's occupational role and attitudes toward children. *American Journal of Orthopsychiatry* 22:366–78.
Atkinson, J. W. (ed.) 1958. *Motives in fantasy, action, and society.* Princeton, N. J.: Van Nostrand.

Blalock, Jr., H. M. 1960. *Social statistics.* New York: McGraw-Hill.

Crocket, H. J. 1962. The achievement motive and differential occupational mobility in the United States. *American Sociological Review* 21:191–204.

Elder, G. H. 1962. *Adolescent achievement and mobility aspirations.* Chapel Hill, N. C.: Institute for Research in Social Science.

Elder, G. H. 1965. Family structure and educational attainment. *American Sociological Review* 30:81–96.

Elder, G. H. 1968. Achievement motivation and intelligence in occupational mobility: A longitudinal analysis. *Sociometry* 31:327–54.

Hammond, S. B. 1954. Class and family. In Ceser and Hammond (eds.), *Social structure and personality in a city.* London: Routledge Kegan. Pp. 238–48.

Kohn, M. L. 1959. Social class and parental values. *American Journal of Sociology:* 64:337–51.

Komarovsky, M. 1962. *Blue collar marriage.* New York: Random House.

McClelland, D. C. 1961. *The achieving society.* Princeton, N. J.: Van Nostrand.

McClelland, D. C.; J. W. Atkinsons; R. A. Clark; and B. L. Lowell. 1953. *The achievement motive.* New York: Appleton-Century-Crofts.

McClelland, D. C.; J. W. Atkinsons; R. A. Clark; and B. L. Lowell. 1958. A scoring manual for the achievement motive. In Atkinson (ed.), *Motives in fantasy, action, and society.* Princeton, N. J.: Van Nostrand.

McKinely, D. 1964. *Social class and family life.* Glencoe, Ill.: The Free Press.

Miller, D., and G. E. Swanson. 1958. *The changing American parent.* New York: Wiley.

Mills, C. W. 1951. *White collar: The American middle class.* New York: Oxford University Press.

Pearlin, L. I., and M. L. Kohn. 1966. Social class, occupation, and parental values: A cross national study. *American Sociological Review* 31: 466–79.

Presthus, R. 1962. *The organizational society.* New York: Random House.

Riesman, D. 1950. *The lonely crowd.* New Haven: Yale University Press.

Rosen, B. C. 1956. The achievement syndrome: A psychocultural dimension of social stratification. *American Sociological Review* 21:203–11.

Rosen, B. C. 1959. Race, ethnicity and the achievement syndrome. *American Sociological Review* 24:47–60.

Rosen, B. C. 1961. Family structure and achievement motivation. *American Sociological Review* 26:574–85.

Rosen, B. C. 1962. Socialization and achievement motivation in Brazil. *American Sociological Review* 27:612–24.

Rosen, B. C. 1964. The achievement syndrome and economic growth in Brazil. *Social Forces* 42:341–54.

Rosen, B. C., and R. D'Andrade. 1959. The psychosocial origins of achievement motivation. *Sociometry* 22:574–85.

Schumpeter, J. A. 1934. *The theory of economic development.* Cambridge, Mass.: Harvard University Press.

Strodbeck, F. 1958. Family interaction, values, and achievement. In McClelland, et al., *Talent and society.* New York: Van Nostrand. Pp. 82–104.

Winterbottom, M. 1958. The relation of need for achievement to learning experiences in independence and mastery. In Atkinson (ed.), *Motives in fantasy, action, and society.* New York: Van Nostrand. Pp. 79–94.

9

Influence of Brothers and Sisters on Sex-Role Behavior

GERALD S. LEVENTHAL

Several investigators (Brim, 1958; Sutton-Smith & Rosenberg, 1965) of sex-role development in two-child families maintain that children in the same family tend to acquire each other's characteristics. They propose that a male will acquire feminine response tendencies from a sister and masculine response tendencies from a brother. Consequently, males with a sister are expected to display a more feminine behavior pattern than males with a brother. This proposition, which assumes that siblings adopt each other's behavior, may be conveniently labeled the imitation hypothesis.

Available research seems consistent with the imitation hy-

Gerald S. Leventhal, "Influence of Brothers and Sisters on Sex-Role Behavior," *Journal of Personality and Social Psychology* 16, no. 3 (1970): 452–65. Copyright 1970 by the American Psychological Association, and reproduced by permission. Footnotes have been renumbered.

Parts of this work were supported by a grant from the United States Office of Education, administered through the Center for Occupational Education at North Carolina State University. The report is a modified version of a symposium paper presented at the 1968 meeting of the American Psychological Association in San Francisco. The author wishes to thank James Goodnight and Donald Drewes for their help in matters of computer programming and statistical procedure and Donald Beale, Donald Draper, Robert Alexander. Donald Knowles, and Adrian Lund for their clerical assistance.

pothesis. For example, Brim (1958) reanalyzed data from Koch's study of 5- and 6-year-old children from two-child families (Koch, 1954, 1955a, 1955b, 1956a, 1956b, 1956c, 1956d, 1956e) and concluded that boys with sisters are more feminine and less masculine than boys with brothers, particularly among the second-borns. Rosenberg and Sutton-Smith (1964) studied game preferences of children of ages 9–12 and found that among boys with one sibling, boys with sisters displayed more feminine preferences than boys with brothers. Sutton-Smith and Rosenberg (1965) administered the *Mf* scale of the MMPI to introductory psychology students. Among men with one sibling, they found that men with sisters displayed a more feminine response pattern than men with brothers, particularly when the men were second-borns. These investigations indicate that the imitation hypothesis holds true for males with one sibling. At all age levels, males with sisters seem more feminine than males with brothers. However, Leventhal (1965) has reported findings inconsistent with the imitation hypothesis. A femininity scale was administered to a sample similar to that studied by Sutton-Smith and Rosenberg (1965), but opposite results were obtained. Men with sisters displayed a less feminine response pattern than men with brothers, particularly among the second-borns. This finding suggests there may be some tendency for a younger male child to adopt characteristics opposite those of his older sibling. Such a tendency would cause a male with a sister to display a less feminine behavior pattern than a male with a brother. This view is in direct contradiction to the imitation hypothesis and may be conveniently labeled the contrast hypothesis. The contrast hypothesis assumes that the presence of a sister leads to the development of an especially masculine male.

   The discrepancy between Leventhal's (1965) findings and investigations which support the imitation hypothesis has generated the studies reported in this paper. Study 1 presents data which contradict the findings of Sutton-Smith and Rosenberg (1965). An explanation for the discrepancy between the two sets of data is then presented. It is suggested that the imitation hypothesis holds true for some trait dimensions, while the contrast hypothesis holds true for others. Studies 2, 3, and 4 support this proposition with results obtained from more than 2,300 males with one sibling.

STUDY 1

Subjects and Procedure

A 38-item Femininity scale drawn from the California Psychological Inventory[1] (Gough, 1957), or CPI, was administered in introductory psychology classes at the University of California, Los Angeles, in the spring and fall of 1964.[2] With twins excluded, there were 218 men with one sibling in the sample. The mean age of these subjects was slightly below 19 years. The mean difference in age between subjects and their siblings was 4.6 years. However, the difference in age was significantly greater among second-born subjects (5.2 years) than among first-born subjects (4.0 years).

Results

Mean scores on the Femininity scale are shown in Table 1. A score of 38 indicates a maximum degree of femininity, a score of 0, a minimum degree. The data were analyzed with a 2 x 2 factorial analysis of variance for unweighted means (Winer, 1962). The main effect of sex of sibling is significant ($F = 4.45$, $p < .05$), but the interaction term and main effect of birth order are not. A specific comparison among the second-borns indicated that men with an older sister obtained significantly less feminine scores than men with an older brother ($F = 4.21$, $p < .05$). Among the first-borns, the comparable difference was nonsignificant. Analysis of covariance was used to partial out effects of age difference on femininity scores. In this analysis, the effects of sex of sibling remained significant, and the proportion of within-cell

---

[1] With permission of Consulting Psychologists Press, Incorporated.

[2] Data obtained during the spring semester have been reported in a paper by Leventhal (1965).

variance accounted for by the age difference covariable was only one-quarter of one per cent.[3]

TABLE 1
MEAN FEMININITY SCORES

S's birth order	Type of sibling	
	Brother	Sister
1st	15.47	14.76
	(47)	(66)
2nd	16.39	14.83
	(59)	(46)

Note.—n for each cell is shown in parentheses. High scores indicate high femininity.

Discussion

On the Femininity scale of the CPI, men with sisters obtained less feminine scores than men with brothers, particularly among the second-borns. This result contradicts the findings of Sutton-Smith and Rosenberg (1965), who used the Mf scale of the MMPI and found an opposite result. The contradiction probably occurs because the CPI Femininity scale and MMPI Mf scale give different weights to various aspects of masculine and feminine behavior. The two scales are composed of a heterogeneous collection of items, which taps a cluster of diverse trait dimensions, rather than a unidimensional trait (Gough, 1957; Hathaway & McKinley, 1951; Little, 1949). It is therefore possible that the CPI Femininity scale gives high weight to trait dimensions for which the contrast hypothesis holds true, while

[3]Scores on the CPI Femininity scale were also obtained for 224 women with one sibling, and an analysis comparable to that for the data shown in Table 1 was performed. Neither the main effects, the interaction term, nor specific comparisons for these data approached statistical significance. This result indicates that the findings reported in this work may hold true only for male populations. Unfortunately, definitive conclusions about this question were not possible in the present work. In Studies 2, 3, and 4 data were gathered at universities in which the overwhelming majority of students were male. The number of women with one sibling was too small to permit meaningful analysis.

the MMPI *Mf* scale gives high weight to trait dimensions for which the imitation hypothesis holds true. Consequently, when men with an older sister are compared to those with an older brother, men with an older sister obtain less feminine scores on the CPI Femininity scale (contrast) and more feminine scores on the MMPI *Mf* scale (imitation).

The studies reported below test the assumptions used to account for the discrepancy between the findings of Study 1 and those of Sutton-Smith and Rosenberg (1965). Studies 2 and 3 identify trait dimensions for which the contrast hypothesis holds true and others for which the imitation hypothesis holds true. Using these results as a guide, Study 4 involves a partitioning of items comprising the MMPI *Mf* scale into several clusters. One cluster of items was expected to yield data consistent with the contrast hypothesis, while another was expected to yield data consistent with the imitation hypothesis.

The three studies reported below employ a 2 x 2 factorial design like that used in Study 1, in which sex of sibling and birth order are independent variables. In each study, a large number of measures were subjected to statistical analysis. Such a procedure increases the likelihood that significant effects will be obtained by chance, and that chance differences will be mistaken for true differences. To reduce the severity of this problem, the measures within each study were classified as either major or supplementary dependent variables. Measures were classified as major dependent variables when they tapped trait dimensions for which the contrast and imitation hypotheses seemed to yield clear predictions. By restricting the size of the pool of theoretically relevant dependent variables, it was hoped to reduce the number of significant chance effects which would be mistaken for findings of theoretical importance. However, data from supplementary dependent variables were analyzed for exploratory purposes.

The number of statistical tests performed would nearly be doubled if the main effect and simple effects of birth order were tested in every instance. However, the independent variable of birth order is actually irrelevant to the major theoretical concerns of this study, except insofar as it may interact with and alter the effect of sex of sibling. Tests of its effects were therefore unnecessary. Nevertheless, because many readers may be interested in birth order, statistical tests of its effects were performed. At appropriate intervals throughout the article, the results of these tests as well as those for supplementary dependent variables are reported in footnotes without further comment.

Criteria for selecting major dependent variables were obtained from literature which identifies trait dimensions that differentiate the sexes (Kagan, 1964; Terman & Miles, 1936; Terman & Tyler, 1954). The following generalizations about sex-role behavior guided the selection of major dependent variables. Among the culturally approved patterns of interest and behavior which are commonly associated with "maleness" are liking for athletic and outdoor activities, great physical strength and athletic ability, liking for mechanical and technical activities, and disinterest in aesthetic and artistic activities. With regard to emotional behavior, more masculine males are expected to suppress emotions such as fear and anxiety, avoid excessive sentimentality, and display a generally lower level of emotional reactivity than women. Among the interpersonal behaviors which are considered appropriate for the more masculine individual are social assertiveness and interpersonal dominance. In addition, examination of typical masculinity-femininity scales suggests that men with more masculine behavior patterns prefer types of social interaction prevalent in all-male peer groups and seek membership in such groups. This list of sex-role behaviors associated with low femininity and high masculinity is not comprehensive, but it does include many of the behavior dimensions assessed in the studies reported below.

STUDY 2

Subjects and Procedure

Subjects were drawn from freshman classes entering North Carolina State University in the fall of 1964 and 1965. Information obtained from admissions application forms submitted by all incoming students was used to identify men with one sibling and to determine sex of sibling and birth order. A total of 1,352 men were studied.[4] Their mean age was slightly greater than 18$\frac{1}{2}$ years. (The difference in age between subjects and their siblings was unknown, because the exact age of siblings was not available.) The admissions application also listed subjects' choice of curriculum, their two most-preferred occupations, and their fathers' occupations and education. A "Student Activities and Interests" sheet was also available for each subject. In filling out this sheet, students examined a list of 30 extracurricular interests and activities and placed a check next to those of special interest to them. Other questions required students to indicate whether they were interested in joining a social fraternity, the number of musical instruments they could play, and whether they sang. For 1,079 students in the sample, records of the Department of Physical Education provided information about athletic performance. Incoming freshman are usually required to take a physical education placement test which includes three measures of motor fitness (chins, push-ups, and vertical jumps) and a multiple-choice test of health knowledge. Students are also tested for swimming ability and classified on a 5-point scale ranging from Beginner 1 to Instructor. Other records provided self-reports of height and weight.

Excluding choice of occupation and choice of curriculum, statistical tests were performed on 36 indexes. Nine of these were regarded as major dependent variables because they tapped trait dimensions for which the contrast and imitation hypotheses yielded opposing predictions. The remaining 27 measures which are described in Footnote 6 were regarded as supplementary dependent variables. Neither the imitation nor contrast hypothesis suggested a clear prediction for them. With respect to measures of occupational choice and curriculum choice, three occupations and two curricula were chosen often enough to permit meaningful chi-square analysis. However, within this group, only the curriculum and occupation of "engineering" was considered a major dependent variable.

[4]The number of records for women with one sibling was too small to permit meaningful analysis.

Results and Discussion

Outdoor interests and athletic skill. The contrast hypothesis suggests that men with sisters display stronger interest in outdoor activities and greater athletic skill than men with brothers. Three outdoor activities were included in the list of extracurricular interests, namely, camping and hiking, horseback riding, and water skiing. An index of outdoor interest was obtained by summing each subject's responses to these items. Values on the index ranged from 0 (not interested in any of the outdoor activities) to 3 (interested in all of them). Two measures of athletic skill were also available, namely, Motor Fitness Index 1 of the Indiana Motor Fitness Test (see Mathews, 1963) and aquatic classification. Scores on the Motor Fitness Index are based on the number of chins and push-ups an individual can perform and the maximum height he attains in the vertical jump. The better the individual's performance, the higher his score on the index.[5] The data were analyzed with 2 x 2 factorial analyses of variance for unweighted means.

Mean responses on the index of outdoor interest are shown in Table 2. A significant main effect of sex of sibling is present ($F = 4.69$, $p < .05$), but the interaction between sex of sibling and birth order is also significant ($F = 5.93$, $p < .05$). Among the first-borns, sex of sibling has no effect. However, among the second-borns, men with older sisters expressed greater interest in outdoor activities than men with older brothers ($F = 8.79$, $p < .01$).

Mean responses on the Motor Fitness Index are presented in Table 3. The main effect of sex of sibling and the interaction term were nonsignificant. However, men with older sisters did obtain significantly higher motor fitness scores than men with older brothers ($F = 4.99$, $p < .05$). The corresponding difference among

[5]Scores on the Motor Fitness Index are derived by converting the individual's performance score on each of the three motor-performance tasks to a standard score and then combining the scale scores as follows:
Motor Fitness Index 1 =

$$\frac{\text{(chins scaled + push-ups scaled)} \times \text{(vertical jump scaled)}}{100}$$

Motor Fitness Index 1 has been shown to correlate highly with a 12-item motor-performance battery which includes measures of strength, speed, endurance, and motor ability (Mathews, 1963).

TABLE 2
MEAN INTEREST IN OUTDOOR ACTIVITIES:
CAMPING AND HIKING, HORSEBACK
RIDING, AND WATER SKIING

S's birth order	Type of sibling	
	Brother	*Sister*
1st	1.27	1.26
	(366)	(451)
2nd	1.20	1.46
	(261)	(274)

Note.—*n* for each cell is shown in parentheses. Mean of 3 indicates interest in all activities; 0 indicates interest in none.

TABLE 3
MEAN SCORES ON INDIANA MOTOR FITNESS
TEST INDEX 1

S's birth order	Type of sibling	
	Brother	*Sister*
1st	60.91	61.10
	(290)	(371)
2nd	59.61	66.78
	(209)	(209)

Note.—*n* for each cell is shown in parentheses. High scores indicate high fitness.

the first-borns was nonsignificant. The index of swimming ability yielded a similar pattern of results, but the tendency for men with older sisters to attain higher scores only reached the .10 level of confidence.

Because body size is correlated with motor performance (Mathews, 1963), there was a possibility that differences on the Motor Fitness Index were mediated by differences in height and weight. To check this possibility, analyses of covariance were performed for the Motor Fitness Index and aquatic classification, using self-reports of height and weight as covariables. When the measure of motor fitness was adjusted for height and weight, the results were somewhat weaker than with height and weight ignored. Nevertheless, the difference between men with older sisters and men with older brothers on the Motor Fitness Index remained significant ($F = 3.86$, $p < .05$). In a similar analysis for the measure of swimming ability, the difference between the two groups of second-born men drew nearer to statistical significance ($F = 3.31$, $p < .10$). It may be concluded that differences in height and weight are not primary mediators of the effect of sex of sibling on athletic skill.

Among the second-borns, results for measures of outdoor interest and athletic skill were consistent with the contrast hypothesis. Men with older sisters displayed greater athletic competence and interest in outdoor activities than men with older brothers. However, among the first-borns, sex of sibling had no clear effect.

Interest in technical activities.   Table 4 shows the percentage of subjects in each group who listed engineering as an occupational preference. Since choice of engineering as an occupation is positively correlated with level of masculinity (Strong, 1959; Terman & Miles, 1936), the contrast hypothesis suggests men with sisters will be more likely to choose engineering as a vocation than men with brothers. The data were analyzed with a chi-square technique described by Rao (1952, pp. 210–14).

TABLE 4
PERCENTAGE OF SUBJECTS IN EACH GROUP LISTING
ENGINEERING AS A PREFERRED OCCUPATION

	Type of sibling	
S's birth order		
	Brother	*Sister*
1st	63.34	60.66
	(341)	(427)
2nd	54.47	63.88
	(246)	(263)

Note.—n for each cell is shown in parentheses. The total N is smaller than in Table 2 because 75 men did not list an occupational preference.

The proportion of men listing engineering in each cell was subjected to an arc-sine transformation, and values of chi-square were computed for the main effect and simple effects of sex of sibling and the interaction effect. The interaction effect was significant ($\chi^2 = 4.65$, $p < .05$), but the main effect of sex of sibling was not. Among the second-borns, men with older sisters were more likely to choose engineering as an occupation than men with older brothers ($\chi^2 = 4.67$, $p < .05$). Among the first-borns the difference was nonsignificant and in the opposite direction. A similar pattern of results occurred with respect to choice of engineering as a curriculum. Among men with older sisters, 58.3 per cent chose engineering as compared to 48.8 per cent of men with older brothers ($\chi^2 = 4.77$, $p < .05$). Results consistent with these findings were obtained on two additional measures. Men with older sisters were significantly more likely to express interest in the extracurricular activities of "Hi-Fi and stereo equipment study" ($\chi^2 = 4.57$, $p < .05$) and "radio station" ($\chi^2 = 5.88$, $p < .05$). On both measures, the corresponding difference among the first-borns was in the same direction, but of considerably smaller magnitude. On the radio station item there was also a significant main effect of sex of sibling.

Attraction to all-male peer groups. For males entering college, the social fraternity is likely to be a highly salient all-male peer group. Consequently, the contrast hypothesis suggests that men with sisters will be more interested in joining a social fraternity than men with brothers. Table 5 indicates subjects' response to the question, "Are you interested in a social fraternity?" Cell entries show the percentage of subjects checking the "yes" alternative in each group. The data were analyzed with the chi-square technique described above. The main effect of sex of sibling is significant ($\chi^2 = 5.46$, $p < .05$), and the interaction effect

TABLE 5
PERCENTAGE OF SUBJECTS IN EACH GROUP EXPRESSING
INTEREST IN JOINING A SOCIAL FRATERNITY

	Type of sibling	
S's birth order	*Brother*	*Sister*
1st	21.64 (365)	23.61 (449)
2nd	20.69 (261)	31.62 (272)

Note.—*n* for each cell is shown in parentheses.

approaches significance ($\chi^2 = 3.30$, $p < .10$). The proportion of individuals interested in fraternity membership is greater among men with older sisters than among men with older brothers ($\chi^2 = 8.32$, $p < .01$). Among the first-borns, the comparable difference is nonsignificant and of considerably smaller magnitude.

Interest in joining a social fraternity is assumed to measure attraction to all-male peer groups, rather than a generalized affiliative tendency. Some support for this interpretation is provided by data from a supplementary dependent measure which asked subjects to list the clubs and organizations to which they belonged. The number of groups listed by men with older sisters tended to be smaller than the number listed by other subjects. This result is consistent with the view that the relatively high frequency of interest in social fraternities among men with older sisters reflects an affiliative tendency which is specific to groups of that type.

Aesthetic interests.   The contrast hypothesis suggests that men with sisters display lower interest in aesthetic activities than men with brothers. Three indicators of aesthetic interest were used. The first was obtained by summing subjects' responses to five areas of extracurricular activity, namely theater, art exhibit preparation, sculpture, painting and sketching, and creative writing. Values on this index ranged from 0 (no interest) to 5 (high interest). Men with older sisters obtained a lower score on this index than any other group, but the differences were nonsignificant. Another measure was provided by an item which asked subjects to indicate the musical instruments they played. There were no significant differences in the number of musical instruments listed. A third measure was obtained from responses to the question, "Do you sing?" Contrary to the contrast hypothesis, the percentage of individuals answering in the affirmative was significantly greater among men with older sisters than among men with older brothers. (The main effect of sex of sibling was also significant.) Thus, data concerning the relationship between sex of sibling and aesthetic interests are contradictory and inconclusive.

On the whole, the results of Study 2 support the contrast

hypothesis. On several trait dimensions, men with older sisters display behaviors opposite those their older siblings are likely to possess. Men with older sisters display a more masculine behavior pattern than men with older brothers on measures of outdoor interest, athletic skill, technical interest, and attraction to all-male peer groups.[6]

[6]There were no significant main effects of birth order on measures of outdoor interest, athletic ability, technical interest, aesthetic interest, and attraction to all-male peer groups. However, several simple effects of birth order were significant. Among men with sisters, the second-borns obtained significantly higher scores than the first-borns on the index of outdoor interest, Motor Fitness Index 1, aquatic classification, interest in fraternity membership, and the question about singing. Among men with brothers, the second-borns chose engineering as an occupation significantly less often than the first-borns.

On the 27 supplementary dependent variables, there were six significant main effects of birth order. Compared with the second-borns, first-born individuals obtained higher grades on a multiple-choice test of health knowledge, listed a larger number of memberships in clubs and organizations, and were more likely to express interest in the extracurricular activities of "reading and discussion of books," "school yearbook," and "stamp and coin collecting." On the other hand, the first-borns were significantly less likely than the second-borns to express interest in the extracurricular activity of bridge playing. For one extracurricular activity, a significant simple effect of birth order was obtained in the absence of a significant main effect. Among men with sisters, fewer first-borns than second-borns displayed interest in "billiards." A significant main effect of sex of sibling was obtained for the occupational choice of architect. Men with brothers listed architecture as a preferred occupation more often than men with sisters. On self-reports of height, there was a small but significant tendency for men with sisters to be shorter than men with brothers. A significant interaction effect which was difficult to interpret was obtained for the extracurricular activity of "chess and checkers." No significant effects of any kind were obtained on self-reports of weight, frequency of church membership, indexes of father's occupational and educational level, or for the extracurricular activities of "record collecting," "film projectionist," "photography," "metal craft," "woodworking," "table tennis," "bowling," "YMCA," "group leadership training," and "international relations." Also, there were no significant effects for the occupation of teaching or curricula related to agriculture. For four extracurricular activities and for a large number of occupations and curricula which were chosen infrequently, the population was too homogeneous to permit a meaningful chi-square analysis, that is, the frequency of "yes" responses was very close to 0 or to 1 (see McNemar, 1955). This group of items included the activities of "debating," "ceramics," "school newspaper," "newspaper, radio and TV publicity"; occupations such as chemist, physicist, mathematician, business manager, and salesman; and curricula such as textiles, architecture, physics, chemistry, and biology. Data for the occupations of farmer and forester and the curriculum of forestry also fell in this category which was unfortunate because the contrast and imitation hypotheses yielded clear predictions for these three choices.

STUDY 3

Subjects and Procedure

Questionnairs were administered in introductory psychology classes at North Carolina State University in four successive semesters. Data of individuals with step-siblings, half-siblings or twin siblings were dropped from the sample. The IPAT Anxiety Scale (Cattell & Scheier, 1963) and Maudsley Personality Inventory (Eysenck & Knapp, 1962) were administered during the fall of 1965 and spring of 1966.[7] In these two semesters, there were 145 males with one sibling. The mean age of these subjects was 20.2 years. The mean difference in age between subjects and their siblings was 4.3 years overall and ranged from 4.9 years for men with younger brothers to 3.7 years for men with younger sisters. No significant effects were obtained on an analysis of variance for age difference scores.

A 28-item Dominance scale taken from the Edwards Personal Preference Schedule[8] or EPPS (Edwards, 1959), and a 46-item Dominance scale taken from the CPI (Gough, 1957) were administered during the fall of 1966 and spring of 1967. In these two semesters, there were 196 males with one sibling.[9] The mean age of these subjects was 19.9 years. The mean difference in age between subjects and their siblings was 4.4 years. It ranged from 4.2 to 4.7 years in the four groups, and none of the differences in age difference approached significance. The anxiety and dominance measures were the major dependent variables of Study 3.

[7]The author is grateful to Elizabeth Carr-Harris and Lynne Siebert, who administered these scales and made their data available for further analysis.

[8]Reproduced by permission of The Psychological Corporation (Copyright 1953) with the proviso that the following notice appear in any written report:

Since there is evidence to indicate that item responses obtained to selected items isolated from the context of a personality inventory may not be comparable to those obtained within the context, the results of this research should not be considered applicable to the standardized complete form of the inventory.

[9]For both the anxiety and dominance measures, the number of females with one sibling was too small to permit meaningful analysis.

However, data were also obtained for 21 supplementary dependent variables which are described in Footnote 10.

Results and Discussion

The imitation hypothesis suggests that men with sisters display greater anxiety and emotional reactivity than men with brothers. Relevant data are presented in Table 6. On both scales,

TABLE 6
MEAN SCORES ON MEASURES OF ANXIETY

Scale	S's birth order	Type of sibling	
		Brother	Sister
IPAT Anxiety Scale*	1st	29.34 (38)	27.02 (51)
	2nd	22.12 (25)	29.06 (31)
Maudsley Neuroticism scale**	1st	24.39 (38)	21.62 (50)
	2nd	18.88 (25)	26.90 (31)

Note.—n for each cell is shown in parentheses.
*High score indicates high anxiety.
**High score indicates high neuroticism.

an analysis of variance for unweighted means yields a nonsignificant main effect of sex of sibling and a significant interaction effect (on the IPAT scale, F for interaction = 5.74, $p < .05$; on the Neuroticism scale, F for interaction = 8.88, $p < .01$). Specific comparisons indicate that men with older sisters express greater anxiety and emotional reactivity than men with older brothers on both the IPAT Anxiety Scale ($F = 5.27$, $p < .05$) and the Maudsley Neuroticism scale ($F = 8.05$, $p < .01$). Among the first-borns the effect of sex of sibling was nonsignificant and in the opposite direction. For the most part, this pattern of results is consistent with findings obtained by Sutton-Smith and Rosenberg (1965) and Rosenberg and Sutton-Smith (1964). Men with older sisters display a more feminine response pattern on anxiety measures than men with older brothers, a result consistent with the imitation hypothesis.

The imitation hypothesis suggests that men with sisters obtain lower dominance scores than men with brothers. Table 7 presents relevant data. On both scales the main effect of sex of sibling is nonsignificant. However, among the first-borns, there is a significant simple effect of sex of sibling. Men with younger sisters obtain lower dominance scores than men with younger brothers on the CPI Dominance scale ($F = 8.14$, $p < .01$) and the EPPS Dominance scale ($F = 6.52$, $p < .05$). Although the interaction term is significant, only on the CPI scale ($F = 4.04$, $p < .05$), sex of sibling appears to have no effect on dominance scores among the second-borns. The finding that men with younger sisters display a less dominant, less masculine response pattern than men with younger brothers is consistent with the imitation hypothesis. However, the result is unusual in that sex of sibling typically has greater impact among the second-borns than among the first-borns. This feature of the relationship between sex of sibling and dominance scores indicates that the relation-

TABLE 7
MEAN SCORES ON MEASURES OF DOMINANCE

Scale	S's birth order	Type of sibling	
		Brother	Sister
CPI Dominance scale *	1st	29.44 (61)	25.98 (56)
	2nd	27.51 (43)	27.91 (35)
EPPS Dominance scale *	1st	13.95 (61)	12.09 (57)
	2nd	13.40 (43)	13.43 (35)

Note.—n for each cell is shown in parentheses.
* High score indicates high dominance.

ship may have a different developmental basis than other findings reported in this study.[10]

STUDY 4

Earlier it was suggested that the imitation hypothesis holds true for some trait dimensions which differentiate the sexes, while the contrast hypothesis holds true for others. One implication of this suggestion is that measures of masculinity such as the MMPI *Mf* scale or CPI Femininity scale can be subdivided into three components or item clusters, namely a cluster of items for which the imitation hypothesis holds true, one for which the

[10]The effects of birth order on the major dependent variables were as follows. On the anxiety scales, the main effect of birth order was nonsignificant, but several simple effects were significant. On both scales, among men with brothers, the first-borns obtained significantly higher scores than the second-borns. Also, on the Maudsley Neuroticism scale, men with older sisters obtained significantly higher scores than men with younger sisters. On the dominance scales, the main effect and simple effects of birth order were nonsignificant.

On the 21 supplementary dependent variables, there were three significant main effects of birth order. Two of these concerned dating behavior. When asked to report the age at which they had first started dating frequently, first-born men reported a mean age of 15.99 years, as compared to 15.36 years for second-born men ($F=11.21$, $p<.01$). Also, the first-borns were significantly less likely than the second-borns to state they had started dating at an earlier age than most persons. There were no significant effects of sex of sibling on these items. Significant main effects of birth order and of sex of sibling were obtained on a question which asked subjects to indicate the number of disagreements and arguments they had with their sibling during an average month in the past when both lived at home. Men with brothers reported a larger number of disagreements and arguments than men with sisters, and first-borns reported a larger number than second-borns. On the Extraversion scale of the Maudsley Inventory, men with older brothers obtained significantly higher scores than men with younger brothers. No significant differences were found on 12 Likert-type items which assessed subjects' beliefs about psychological differences between the sexes and about the "proper" social role of women. There were also no clear results on four items concerning sleeping habits and one concerning tolerance for pain.

A further analysis was carried out to detect possible effects of difference in age between subjects and their siblings. Within each of the four groups of subjects, polynomial regression analysis was applied to all dependent variables. In a search for significant linear or higher order curvilinear relationships, these analyses were carried out up to and including the sixth order for each dependent variable. However, the proportion of variance accounted for by these curve-fitting procedures was rarely sufficient to attain statistical significance. In addition, there was no clear pattern among the few scattered significant effects that were obtained.

contrast hypothesis holds true, and a residual cluster of items for which neither hypothesis holds true. On the contrast component, men with older sisters would be expected to obtain less feminine scores than men with older brothers. On the imitation component, men with older sisters would be expected to obtain more feminine scores. A prerequisite for testing these predictions is the availability of criteria for assigning specific test items to the appropriate item cluster. The results of Studies 2 and 3 provide tentative criteria for such assignment.

Subjects and Procedure

The subjects were 644 male students at the University of North Carolina at Chapel Hill. As part of a large-scale testing program, the MMPI (Dahlstrom & Welsh, 1960; Hathaway & McKinley, 1951) was administered to all incoming freshmen for several years. For freshmen entering in the fall of 1966, information about age and sex of siblings was also gathered.[11] There were 564 males with one sibling in this group. In addition, information obtained from several introductory psychology classes in the spring of 1967 made it possible to identify 80 additional men who had one sibling and had completed the MMPI. The two subsamples were combined. The mean age for all subjects was 18.3 years. The mean difference in age between subjects and their siblings was quite similar for subjects in the different birth order and sex of sibling categories, and ranged from 4.4 to 4.7 years, with an overall mean of 4.5 years.

Each subject's item-by-item response to the MMPI was available on IBM punch cards. Most subjects had taken an abbreviated form of the inventory, in which 109 items were deleted from the final third of the test. However, all questions in the *Mf* scale were administered in their usual context because there were no item deletions from among the first 367 items of the inventory.

The 60 items of the MMPI *Mf* scale were examined carefully by the author, who judged each item and assigned it to the

[11]The author is grateful to Clifford Reiffler and Stuart Valins, who gathered these data and made them available for further analysis. The number of records for women with one sibling was too small to permit meaningful analysis.

imitation, contrast, or residual component. At the time these judgmental classifications were made, the author had no knowledge of the results for specific items or for particular groups of items. The imitation component consisted of 13 items which the author judged to be measures of anxiety level and emotional reactivity.[12] The contrast component consisted of 25 items which assess trait dimensions such as interest in outdoor activities, interest in technical and mechanical activities, interest in the social activities of all-male peer groups, sex-related occupational preferences, disinterest in aesthetic activities, and a number of other behaviors which the author considered likely to fit with this cluster.[13] The residual component consisted of the remaining 22 items in the *Mf* scale, which assess an assortment of characteristics such as sex deviancy, cynicism, aggressiveness, religious interest, and preference for certain childhood activities.

In addition to the total *Mf* scale and its components, scores were computed for Welsh's Factor A Scale (Dahlstrom & Welsh, 1960), the Repression-Sensitization (R-S) Scale (Byrne, 1961, 1964), and the Dominance and Revised Dominance scales (Dahlstrom & Welsh, 1960; Gough, McClosky, & Meehl, 1951). Scores on the Dominance scales were actually partial scores because a few items in the scales were excluded from the abbreviated form of the MMPI that was used. For most subjects, data from Lykken's (1957) measure of emotional reactivity were also available. Finally, for exploratory purposes, scores were computed for 11 of the original MMPI subscales and for 20 additional subscales listed by Dahlstrom and Welsh (1960). Footnote 14 describes most of these supplementary measures. Analyses were also

---

[12]The items in the imitation component were 134T, 179T, 217T, 226T, 239T, 278T, 297T, 299T, 79F, 176F, 214F, 262F, 264F. The letter following each number indicates the feminine response alternative.

[13]The items in the contrast component were 4T, *25T, 77T,* 78T, 87T, 92T, 126T, 132T, 140T, 149T, 203T, *204T, 261T, 1F,* 81F, *99F,* 116F, *120F,* 144F, 219F, *221F, 223F, 229F, 254F,* 283F. The letter following each number indicates the feminine response alternative. Items assessing aesthetic interest were included despite the equivocal results for such measures in Study 2, because scales in inventories such as the Strong Vocational Interest Blank (Strong, 1959) strongly indicate that strength of aesthetic interests is inversely related to the strength of outdoor and technical interests. The 11 italicized items are those found to discriminate most strongly between men with older sisters and men with older brothers.

performed on the supplementary dependent variables of self-reported height and weight and numerical indexes of father's occupational and educational level.

Results and Discussion

Table 8 presents mean scores for all groups on the complete 60-item *Mf* scale of the MMPI. Contrary to the findings of Sutton-Smith and Rosenberg (1965), there were no significant effects of sex of sibling. Scores for men with older sisters were quite similar to those for men with older brothers. Table 9 presents mean scores on the contrast and imitation components of the *Mf* scale. As expected, on the contrast component men with older sisters obtained significantly less feminine scores than men with older brothers ($F = 6.35$, $p < .05$). The main effect of sex of sibling was also significant ($F = 4.08$, $p < .05$), but the interaction term was not. Nevertheless, the influence of sex of sibling among the first-borns appears relatively slight and is nonsignificant. Examination of results for individual items in the contrast component revealed that for 22 of the 25 items, the percentage of subjects choosing the masculine response alternative was greater among men with older sisters than among men with older brothers. (Footnote 13 identifies the more discriminating items.)

On the imitation component of the *Mf* scale, men with older sisters obtained more feminine scores than men with older brothers, but neither the main effect nor the simple effects of sex of sibling were significant. Thus, the difference between the two second-born groups on the imitation component was weaker than expected, although the direction of the difference was opposite that obtained on the contrast component. On the residual component there were no significant effects.

Estimates of the reliability of the 13-item imitation component and 25-item contrast component were obtained with an analysis of variance procedure suggested by Winer (1962, p. 131). For the imitation component, the index r_k (a measure of equivalence between items) assumed a value of .65, which indicates a moderately high degree of consistency across items. For the contrast component, the same index of internal consistency reliability assumed a value of .50, which indicates a somewhat lower degree of homogeneity between items.

TABLE 8
MEAN SCORES ON THE TOTAL *Mf* SCALE OF THE MMPI

S's birth order	Type of sibling	
	Brother	Sister
1st	25.51	25.73
	(180)	(180)
2nd	26.50	26.26
	(136)	(148)

Note.—*n* for each cell is shown in parentheses. High scores indicate high femininity.

TABLE 9
MEAN SCORES ON THE CONTRAST COMPONENT
AND IMITATION COMPONENT OF THE *Mf*
SCALE OF THE MMPI

Subscale	S's birth order	Type of sibling	
		Brother	Sister
Contrast component			
	1st	8.63	8.57
	2nd	9.24	8.37
Imitation component			
	1st	5.82	5.92
	2nd	6.14	6.51

Note.—Cell frequencies are identical to those shown in Tables 8 and 10. High scores indicate high femininity.

TABLE 10
MEAN SCORES ON THE REVISED DOMINANCE
SCALE OF THE MMPI

S's birth order	Type of sibling	
	Brother	Sister
1st	9.12	8.51
	(180)	(180)
2nd	8.82	8.76
	(136)	(148)

Note.—*n* for each cell is shown in parentheses. High scores indicate high dominance.

Results were nonsignificant for Welsh's Factor A, the R-S scale, and Lykken scale, the three measures of emotional reactivity and anxiety level. However, on all three measures men with older sisters obtained higher scores than men with older brothers. This pattern of findings is consistent with that obtained on the imitation component of the *Mf* scale. Results for the Revised Dominance scale are shown in Table 10. Men with younger brothers manifested a significantly higher level of interpersonal dominance than men with younger sisters ($F = 6.40$, $p < .05$). On the older version of the Dominance scale, the corresponding difference reached the .10 level of confidence ($F = 3.02$). On both dominance measures, the main effect of sex of sibling, interaction term, and simple effect of sex of sibling among the second-borns were nonsignificant.[14]

[14]Except for a significant main effect of birth order on the imitation component of the *Mf* scale, all main effects and simple effects of birth order were nonsignificant on the major dependent variables of Study 4. Results for the supplementary dependent measures were as follows. There were no significant effects of any type on 10 of 11 original MMPI subscales. The exception was for the Hypomania scale on which men with younger sisters obtained lower scores than either men with younger brothers or men with older sisters. Significant effects were obtained on four other scales from the MMPI. Men with younger sisters expressed less cynicism, reported less family discord, and obtained lower scores on ego inflation than men with younger brothers. Men with younger sisters also expressed less cynicism, lower ego inflation, and greater shyness than men with older sisters. Significant main effects of sex of sibling were obtained on the family discord and shyness scales. Men with sisters reported greater shyness and less family discord than men with brothers. Results for 16 additional scales drawn from the MMPI were nonsignificant. This group of scales included measures of characteristics such as dependency, ethnocentrism, manifest hostility, originality, ego strength, ego overcontrol, test-taking defensiveness, and Welsh's Factor R. No significant differences were obtained on an index of father's educational level. However, on an index of father's occupational level, there was a significant main effect of birth order. Fathers of first-born individuals had a lower mean occupational level than fathers of second-born individuals. On self-reports of weight there were no significant effects, but on self-reports of height there was a small but significant tendency for men with younger sisters to be taller than men with younger brothers. It should be noted these findings for father's occupational level and self-reports of height are inconsistent with data from similar indexes in Study 2.

To detect possible effects of difference in age between subjects and their siblings, polynomial regression analysis was applied to all dependent measures within each group of subjects. These curve-fitting procedures were carried out up to and including the fifth order, but the proportion of variance accounted for was rarely great enough to attain statistical significance. There was no obvious pattern among those effects that were significant.

The contrast component extracted from the MMPI *Mf* scale yielded results generally consistent with the findings of Studies 1 and 2. Men with older sisters displayed a more masculine response pattern on the component than men with older brothers. Simultaneously, the imitation component of the *Mf* scale yielded results in which the difference between these second-born groups was reversed. Results from measures of anxiety and emotional reactivity do not give clear support to the findings of Study 3 and of Sutton-Smith and Rosenberg (1965), but neither can they be said to disconfirm these findings. Although the obtained differences were nonsignificant, they were in the expected direction. It therefore seems reasonable to stand by the earlier conclusion that men with older sisters display greater anxiety and emotional reactivity than men with older brothers. With respect to dominance scores of first-born individuals, the results were consistent with those of Study 3. Men with younger brothers displayed higher dominance than men with younger sisters.

DISCUSSION AND CONCLUSIONS

The results indicate the existence of both contrast and imitation phenomena in second-born males with one sibling. However, studies of college-age populations examine only the aftereffects of sibling-sibling and parent-child interactions which occurred years earlier. They yield no direct information concerning the family interaction patterns which might cause a younger male to adopt behavior patterns opposite or similar to those of his older sibling. Nevertheless, it is useful to speculate about the developmental origins of results consistent with the contrast hypothesis. Two possible mechanisms which might cause a second-born male to adopt response patterns opposite those of his older sibling are described below. The first is a comparison-prevention mechanism, the second a negative-modeling mechanism. Because many authors (e.g., Bandura, 1962; Brim, 1958) have discussed conditions which might cause a child to imitate his sibling, nothing need be said here concerning the origin of imitation effects.

In families with two male children, the younger boy may frequently adopt a "comparison-prevention strategy," that is, he may adopt behavior patterns opposite those of his older brother to prevent himself from being evaluated unfavorably. On an absolute scale, the younger boy is usually less advanced both physically and mentally. Consequently, he is likely to be judged inferior in comparison to his older brother. Since this evaluation is quite threatening to the younger boy, he will attempt to minimize opportunites for such invidious social comparisons. Festinger's (1954) theory of social comparison suggests that the younger boy could reduce the frequency of unfavorable comparisons by adopting behaviors so different from those of his older brother that it would become difficult to compare them. This mechanism would tend to generate less masculine behavior in the younger child.

A second possible explanation of results consistent with the contrast hypothesis assumes that an older sister serves as a negative model for the younger male child, that is, as someone whose traits he does not adopt because he considers the traits undesirable. Such negative modeling effects would be especially likely to occur after an initial period during which the younger male did imitate his older sister's behavior. To the extent he adopted her feminine response patterns, he would eventually be subjected to disapproval from parents and peers. Such disapproval would motivate him to eliminate and cover over all feminine response tendencies. To the extent he succeeded in modifying his behavior, he would display an especially masculine response pattern. This mechanism may help explain why studies of younger populations (Brim, 1958; Rosenberg & Sutton-Smith, 1964) have obtained results more consistent with the imitation hypothesis than with the contrast hypothesis. At younger age levels, the tendency of the boy to perceive his older sister as a negative model may not yet have been operating long enough or strongly enough to produce complete suppression of the feminine traits he acquired from her.

In most instances the influence of a brother or sister was considerably greater among second-born than among first-born males. This result is consistent with either mechanism described above. It is consistent with the comparison-prevention mechanism because fear of invidious comparison would probably be much stronger in the younger of two male children. There would be little reason for the more competent older child to resort to such a strategy. It is also consistent with the negative-modeling mechanism because the tendency to imitate is contingent upon a model's power (Bandura, 1962). Consequently, a younger child would be more likely to imitate an older sibling than vice versa. Since a first-born male would not imitate a younger sister's behavior, he would not be exposed to subsequent disapproval that would induce him to adopt unusually strong masculine response patterns. There is a third possible explanation of the greater impact of sex of sibling on the second-born. In the first few years of life, the first-born individual is not likely to have a sibling. Consequently, sex of sibling could not affect his development during this early formative period. However, for the second-born individual, the family environment contains an older sibling from the moment the younger child enters the family, and the sex of that older sibling can have a continuing influence throughout the entire course of the younger child's development.

The negative-model and comparison-prevention explanations suggest mechanisms that cause second-born males to adopt response patterns opposite those of their older sibling. However, the existence of findings consistent with the imitation hypothesis indicates that the impact of such mechanisms is limited by the operation of other variables. The task of identifying these limiting variables will be difficult because certain findings which seem consistent with the imitation hypothesis may actually be unrelated to it. A case in point is the finding that men with younger brothers obtained higher dominance scores than men with younger sisters. This result is consistent with the imitation hypothesis, but may actually have more to do with the instrumental value of dominant behavior than with imitation of siblings. (For males with younger brothers, dominant behavior would be especially useful for success in sibling-rivalry conflicts and would therefore be strongly reinforced.) A similar problem of interpretation is posed by the finding that men with older sisters display higher anxiety than men with older brothers. This result is consistent with the imitation hypothesis, but can also be accounted for by the negative-modeling mechanism. A second-born male who adopted his older sister's behavior and was subsequently confronted with disapproval from parents and peers would experience much self-doubt and anxiety. Furthermore, as Sutton-Smith and Rosenberg (1965) have suggested, the conflict between earlier acquired feminine response tendencies and superimposed masculine response tendencies would generate considerable emotional tension. Ultimately, the issues raised by such alternative explanations must be resolved by studies which examine directly family interaction patterns in two-child families and their impact on second-born males.

REFERENCES

Bandura, A. 1962. Social learning through imitation. *Nebraska Symposium on Motivation* 10: 211–69.

Brim, O. G. 1958. Family structure and sex role learning by children: A further analysis of Helen Koch's data. *Sociometry* 21: 1–16.

Byrne, D. 1961. The repression-sensitization scale: Rationale, reliability, and validity. *Journal of Personality* 29: 334–49.

Byrne, D. 1964. Repression-sensitization as a dimension of personality. In B. A. Maher (ed.), *Progress in experimental personality research,* vol. 1. New York: Academic Press.

Cattell, R. B., and I. H. Scheier. 1963. *Handbook for the IPAT anxiety scale questionnaire,* 2nd ed. Champaign, Ill.: Institute for Personality and Ability Testing.

Dahlstrom, W. G., and G. S. Welsh. 1960. *An MMPI handbook.* Minneapolis: University of Minnesota Press.

Edwards, A. L. 1959. *Edwards Personal Preference Schedule manual,* rev. ed. New York: Psychological Corporation.

Eysenck, H. J., and R. R. Knapp. 1962. *The Maudsley personality inventory manual.* San Diego: Educational and Industrial Testing Service.

Festinger, L. 1954. A theory of social comparison processes. *Human Relations* 7: 117–40.

Gough, H. G. 1957. *Manual for the California Psychological Inventory.* Palo Alto: Consulting Psychologists Press.

Gough, H. G.; H. McClosky; and P. E. Meehl. 1951. A personality scale for dominance. *Journal of Abnormal and Social Psychology* 46: 360–66.

Hathaway, S. R., and J. C. McKinley. 1951. *Minnesota Multiphasic Personality Inventory,* rev. ed. New York: Psychological Corporation.

Kagan, J. 1964. Acquisition and significance of sex typing and sex role identity. In M. L. Hoffman and L. W. Hoffman (eds.), *Child development research,* vol. 1. New York: Russell Sage Foundation.

Koch, H. L. 1954. The relation of "primary mental abilities" in five- and six-year-olds to sex of child and characteristics of his sibling. *Child Development* 25: 209–23.

Koch, H. L. 1955a. The relation of certain family constellation characteristics and the attitudes of children toward adults. *Child Development* 26: 13–40.

Koch, H. L. 1955b. Some personality correlates of sex, sibling position, and sex of sibling among five- and six-year-old children. *Genetic Psychology Monographs* 52: 3–50.

Koch, H. L. 1956a. Attitudes of young children toward their peers as related to certain characteristics of their siblings. *Psychological Monographs* 70: (19, whole no. 426).

Koch, H. L. 1956b. Children's work attitudes and sibling characteristics. *Child Development* 27: 289–310.

Koch, H. L. 1956c. Sibling influence on children's speech. *Journal of Speech and Hearing Disorders* 21: 322–28.

Koch, H. L. 1956d. Sissiness and tomboyishness in relation to sibling characteristics. *Journal of Genetic Psychology* 88: 231–44.

Koch, H. L. 1956e. Some emotional attitudes of the young child in relation to characteristics of his sibling. *Child Development* 27: 393–426.

Leventhal, G. S. 1965. Sex of sibling as a predictor of personality characteristics. Paper presented at the meeting of the Southeastern Psychological Association, Atlanta.

Little, J. W. 1949. An analysis of the Minnesota Multiphasic Personality Inventory. M.A. thesis. Chapel Hill: University of North Carolina.

Lykken, D. T. 1957. A study of anxiety in the sociopathic personality. *Journal of Abnormal and Social Psychology* 55: 6–10.

Mathews, D. K. 1963. *Measurement in physical education,* 2nd ed. Philadelphia: Saunders.

McNemar, Q. 1955. *Psychological statistics,* 2nd ed. New York: Wiley.

Rao, C. R. 1952. *Advanced statistical methods in biometric research.* New York: Wiley.

Rosenberg, B. G., and B. Sutton-Smith. 1964. Ordinal position and sex-role identification. *Genetic Psychology Monographs* 70: 297–328.

Strong, E. K. 1959. *Strong vocational interest blank manual.* Palo Alto: Consulting Psychologists Press.

Sutton-Smith, B., and B. G. Rosenberg. 1965. Age changes in the effects of ordinal position on sex-role identification. *Journal of Genetic Psychology* 107: 61–73.

Terman, L. M., and C. C. Miles. 1936. *Sex and personality.* New York: McGraw-Hill.

Terman, L. M., and L. E. Tyler. 1954. Psychological sex differences. In L. Carmichael (ed.), *Manual of child psychology,* 2nd ed. New York: Wiley.

Winer, B. J. 1962. *Statistical principles in experimental design.* New York: McGraw-Hill.

IV

Change and Resocialization

10

Social Structure, Identification and Change in a Treatment-Oriented Institution

RAYMOND J. ADAMEK
and EDWARD Z. DAGER

In recent years, sociologists have focused a good deal of attention on what Goffman (1961) has called the "total institution," and especially on correctional institutions. As these studies have accumulated, our knowledge of the complexity of such institutions and their related subsystems has increased. Earlier studies, such as those of Clemmer (1958), McCorkle and Korn (1958), and Sykes (1958), described what came to be known as the "solidary opposition" model of inmate culture, with inmates aligned almost as one body against the formal organization and its goals. Newcomers to the inmate world were soon socialized into this inmate culture, and the process of "prisonization" was thought to increase with length of incarceration. Wheeler's (1961) study, however, indicated that inmate values tended to follow a U-

Raymond J. Adamek and Edward Z. Dager, "Social Structure, Identification and Change in a Treatment-Oriented Institution," *American Sociological Review* 33, no. 6 (December 1968): 931–44.

The authors wish to express their thanks to the Department of Sociology, Purdue University, for providing travel funds and other expenses incidental to this research.

shaped pattern, being most conventional at the beginning and end of one's sentence. He suggested that those nearing the end of their sentence were experiencing anticipatory socialization which would prepare them for life in the outside world. Garabedian (1963) noted a similar pattern in his study, but also noted that not all prisoners' values changed in the same manner. The type of role one adopted during his incarceration determined in part the extent and point of greatest impact of the prison culture on his initial values.

The relatively simple "solidary opposition" model of inmate culture has now been replaced by a more complex model which finds inmate organization dependent in large part upon the location of the institution's primary goals along a custodial-training-treatment continuum. This development owes much to the work of Vinter and Janowitz (1959), Grusky (1959), Street (1965), and Berk (1966), and has culminated in a volume by Street, Vinter, and Perrow (1967) which reports the results of these and related studies which examine the effect of organizational goals not only on inmate culture, but also on staff-inmate relations, staff-staff relations, staff-parent organization relations, and institution-local community relations.

All of the aforementioned studies have dealt with institutions serving males. Until recent years, comparatively few sociological studies have been made of institutions for females. The work of Heffernan (1964), Ward and Kassebaum (1965), and Giallombardo (1966), however, serves to close this gap. Studying three different institutions serving adult females, they all find pseudo-family and homosexual ties to be an important aspect of inmate social organization, although Heffernan especially notes two other major adaptations to prison life, relating prison roles to criminal career prior to incarceration. Kosofsky and Ellis (1958) and Konopka (1966), among others, note similar patterns in institutions serving adolescent females.

The particular appeal of the correctional institution for the sociologist, of course, is not only that it is a society-in-miniature, whose structure and functioning he may describe, but also that it is what Vinter (1963) has called a "people-changing organization." Such organizations, he points out, "are usually concerned with effecting new and diffuse modes of behavior, new self-images or personalities" in the people who come to it. This they attempt to do by deliberately structuring staff-client relations in a manner intended to permit realization of this goal. Such organizations are, therefore, engaged in the business of socialization, a process of major interest to the sociologist. How successful institutions are at this business will depend not only on their major goal-orientation, but in large part first, upon how aware they are of inmate-inmate relations, and second, upon how successful they are in mobilizing these relations to support the achievement of staff goals. Ohlin and Lawrence (1959) and Vinter (1963) point out the perils of ignoring the inmate culture if treatment goals are to be achieved, and the work of Blum (1962), Fisher (1961), and Polsky (1962) in institutions serving male delinquents lends empirical support to their papers. Cressey (1955), Grosser (1958), and Vinter and Janowitz (1959), among others, have suggested principles which might be followed in order to successfully involve the inmate culture in assisting the staff in the task of socializing the individual inmate. These principles have been put into practice to varying degrees, and have met with more or less success at Northways (Miller, 1964), at Highfields (McCorkle et al., 1958), and in the Provo Experiment (Empey & Rabow, 1961).

IDENTIFICATION

One important factor in understanding why some institutions are able to mobilize inmate support for staff goals, and why some inmates are effectively socialized by their institutional experience, while others are not, is the social-psychological process of identification. Unless the inmates come to accept staff members as significant others, unless they come to feel a part of the institution so that its goals become their goals, we can hardly expect the staff to enlist the aid of the inmate culture, or to be successful in its task of people-changing.[1]

---

[1]Grusky (1962) has indicated that authoritarian inmates in a treatment-oriented correctional camp were most effectively indoctrinated by the staff. Authoritarianism may well be one personality variable which facilitates identification in such settings although we have not as yet explored this relationship in the present study.

We may distinguish at least three types of identification: personal, positional, and institutional. Following Winch's (1962) analysis of the first two types, personal identification signifies that type in which the model becomes a significant other to the identifier, who feels positive affection and admiration for the model, takes on his norms and values, and defines the model's direct control over him as legitimate. Effective socialization within the institution then, would be facilitated if an inmate personally identified with a staff member, or with another inmate who was himself effectively socialized by the institution.

Positional identification is that which results from one individual being placed in a role relationship with another, in which relations are reciprocal, e.g., teacher/student or staff-member/inmate, are governed by norms, and in which the model probably has control over resources valuable to the identifier, and is superior in status to the identifier. The identifier will feel admiration and respect for the model, but not necessarily affection or emotional warmth. Again, a staff member or another inmate might serve as the model for positional identification.

Finally, we may speak of institutional identification, by which we mean that an individual comes to feel a part of an organization, has primarily positive attitudes toward it, and in general has accepted its goals, values, and norms as his own. Institutional identification is closely related to positional identification, since the individual comes into contact with the "institution" through the roles he plays in that institution relative to others within it. It differs in that it is somewhat less dependent upon a specific model in the form of a single individual, and is broader in scope.

The degree to which an individual identifies with a particular organization is not entirely beyond the organization's control, as Etzioni (1961) has pointed out. By focusing on various types of control and reward mechanisms, varying degrees of commitment to the organization may be obtained. Moreover, such factors as the clarity of organizational structure and role expectations, the length of time an individual anticipates membership in an organization and actually spends in the organization, the number of alternative reference groups available to the individual, the degree to which the individual is allowed to participate in organizational activities, and the degree to which it is possible for him to increase his organizational status, all have a bearing on the likelihood that identification will take place, and are, in fact, amenable to control by the organization.[2]

Identification with other persons or groups implies that these persons become significant others to ego, and that these groups become his reference groups. As the individual identifies, therefore, he becomes more amenable to social influence. He looks to those with whom he identifies to define role expectations for him, is sensitive to the sanctions they impose, and receives gratification from pleasing them. They become the primary audience to which he plays his roles. Their norms and values are utilized as criteria for judging his behavior, and in time are adopted as his own.

In view of the foregoing discussion, we hypothesize that both institutional identification and identification with staff members in correctional institutions are directly related to the amount and type of change inmates experience during their incarceration. Further, we suggest that relatively clear organizational structure and role expectations, long length of anticipated and actual stay, few alternative reference groups, high organizational participation, and readily available channels for organizational mobility are conducive to identification with the institution.

PROCEDURE AND DATA

A treatment-oriented,[3] closed institution for delinquent girls provided the setting in which we were able to "test" these hypotheses. The institution is located in a large midwestern city, and is operated by the Sisters of the Good Shepherd, who operate some 48 similar institutions in the country. Together, these institutions are said to serve one-fourth of our delinquent female

[2]For a fuller discussion of the factors conducive to positional identification and a review of some of the pertinent literature, see Adamek (1965).

[3]As will be clear from the description to be given later in the text, the study institution might more accurately be termed a training institution in the Street et al. (1967) sense. However, since it does utilize individual and group counseling sessions which aim at increasing inmates' insight into their behavior, the treatment-oriented label is felt to be appropriate.

population (Engh, 1966). An official brochure describing the institution notes, "The environment [the institution] offers shields the girl from her former associates and from a prejudicial society. It provides opportunities to acquire new ideals and constructive habits that will reestablish her in society." The staff attempts to provide what is felt most of the girls have lacked in their past life—love (a concern for the individual's welfare, and interest in that individual as a person), and firm direction.[4]

Responsibility for the day-to-day management of the institution rests upon the shoulders of one of the nuns, who serves as Directress of Girls and Co-Director of the Diagnostic Center. Two psychiatrists, a psychologist, several doctors and dentists, and a nurse serve on a part-time basis. A full-time Director of Social Service, a part-time social worker, a part-time administrative assistant, and two secretaries round out the diagnostic center staff. The institution also maintains an accredited, four-year high school, staffed by eight nuns and four lay women. Four nuns, including the Directress, serve as "group mothers" to the four school classes, and conduct weekly group meetings, to be described below. The group mothers are in contact with the girls more than any other staff member, and sleep in private rooms within the girls' dorms.

Data on the institution and the girls were gathered by questionnaire, an extensive search of institutional records, informal conversations with staff, structured interviews with 50 of the girls, and non-participant observation in the institution. The principal author spent 55 days at the institution over an eight-month period, including eight days observing the girls in their daily routine. He also attended several special institutional functions, e.g., graduation ceremonies.

The Delinquents

The girls resident at the institution (the normal population is between 80–105) are committed by the Courts. Admission, however, is selective. Only those girls are admitted who are over 13 years of age, have completed at least eight years of schooling, and

[4]For a discussion of the treatment philosophy and program of the Sisters of the Good Shepherd, see Thompson (1961).

who are judged by the staff, on the basis of referral material, to indicate a potential for benefiting from the program. In addition, girls who have severe emotional problems are not admitted, nor are those who are known to have had homosexual experiences.

The 119 girls who were residents sometime between May and October of 1966 comprise the population of the present study.[5] They are predominantly white (86.8 per cent) Protestants (59.7 per cent). One girl is Jewish, 28.6 per cent are Catholic, and 10.9 per cent indicate no religious preference. On the basis of father's occupation, the girls come from predominantly lower-middle and upper-lower class families. Of those whose fathers' occupations were known (information was lacking for 20 girls), approximately 33 per cent were skilled manual workers, 25 per cent were operatives and semi-skilled workers, and 16 per cent were unskilled laborers. Ten per cent of the girls had fathers with occupations above that of clerical worker.

Forty-nine per cent of the girls were admitted to the institution between the ages of thirteen and fifteen-and-a-half, and 51 per cent were older at admission. Their primary offenses were rather typical of female delinquents. Sixteen per cent were specifically charged with ungovernability, 22 per cent with runaway, 7 per cent with truancy, 2 per cent with sex delinquency, and 45 per cent with a combination of these offenses. Five per cent of the girls were charged with stealing, and three per cent were apparently committed to protect them from an undesirable home atmosphere. The girls' records indicated that 40 per cent had no official police contact prior to admission, 27 per cent had one such contact, and 28 per cent had two or more contacts.

Measures of Identification

During the course of a case study of the institution, the senior author administered questionnaires which contained two measures of identification and five measures of change. Identification of the girls with staff members was measured by the Interpersonal Check List (ICL) (Leary, 1956, 1957). This instru-

---

[5]Because of missing data, the N's reported below vary from this total. In particular, 14 girls were released from the institution early in the study before proper coordination could be effected, and most data are missing for these girls.

ment contains 128 adjectives or phrases which the respondent may signify as descriptive of his "real" self, his "ideal" self, or other persons. An individual is said to identify with another if his real-self description is similar to his description of that person. Leary (1956) presents the procedure by which an "identify" or "does-not-identify" decision may be made. In utilizing the ICL, we are assuming that a person who is perceived as similar to oneself is a significant other who will be able to influence one's norms and behavior. The work of Fiedler (1953) and Jourard (1957) lends some support to this assumption.

Identification with the institution was measured by a 35-item Likert scale adapted from a longer scale developed by Eshleman et al. (1960). Sample items from this scale include the following: "I'm glad I came to (institution)," "I feel I really belong to (institution)," and "Anyone who accepts the values of (institution) simply does not think for herself." Utilizing the mean-difference method suggested by Edwards (1957), we found all items discriminated satisfactorily. The corrected split-half reliability of the scale was 0.96. With a possible range of scores from 35 to 175, the actual range for our respondents was 46 to 175. Respondents were divided into three numerically equal groups, and classified as high (score 148 and above), medium (122 to 147), and low (121 and below) identifiers.

As a partial validity check on our measures of identification, we analyzed the relationship between identification and two other variables, leadership and conformity, reasoning that identification with a staff member and with the institution should be positively related to being a leader, and to being high on conformity to institutional norms.[6] The results generally support our expectations. While 35.1 per cent of those ($N=57$) who identify

[6]Girls were classified as leaders if they had served at least once as official group leaders (see text below). A measure of conformity to institutional norms was obtained by dividing the number of gold stars (see text below) a girl had been awarded by the number of months she had resided in the institution. Girls who received 60 per cent or more of their possible gold stars were classified as high conformers, those receiving 30–59 per cent were classified as medium conformers, and those receiving 29 per cent or less were classified as low conformers. These data include only girls resident at the institution for four months or more, since girls were not usually permitted to serve as group leaders before this period, and this was felt to be the minimum time in which a girl could establish a meaningful pattern of conformity.

with staff are leaders, only 17.2 per cent of those ($N=29$) who do not identify are leaders. Since age at entrance to the institution was related to identification with staff members, age differences might have accounted for this finding. However, even when we control for age, those who identify with staff are more likely to be leaders than those who do not identify. Similarly, while 50.0 per cent of those ($N=32$) with high *institutional* identification are leaders, leaders comprise only 25.0 per cent of those ($N=28$) with medium, and 10.7 per cent of those ($N=28$) with low institutional identification. Leaders are more likely to have high institutional identification than nonleaders, even when we control for length of stay, which was found to be significantly related to institutional identification.

Girls who identify with staff, and who are high on institutional identification are also more likely to be high on conformity than those who do not identify. Thus, while 37.5 per cent of those ($N=56$) who identify with staff are high conformers, this is true of 23.3 per cent of those ($N=30$) who do not identify. The trend is maintained when we control for age at entrance. Of those high on institutional identification ($N=33$), 54.5 per cent are high on conformity, 39.4 per cent are medium, and 6.1 per cent are low. Of those ($N=27$) low on institutional identification, 33.3 per cent are high on conformity, 37.0 per cent are medium, and 29.6 per cent are low. The direction of the relationship is maintained when we control for length of stay.

Measures of Change

The ICL, the Minnesota Multiphasic Personality Inventory (MMPI), and the IPAT Anxiety Scale are administered to the girls by the staff as part of normal intake processing. It was therefore decided to readminister these tests to provide a longitudinal measure of change. In view of the institution's goals, and the means it utilizes to reach these goals, we expected that the girls would "improve" on these measures to the extent that they identified with the staff and/or institution.

Besides providing a measure of identification with other persons, the ICL provides a measure of self-esteem, defined operationally as a low self/ideal-self discrepancy score. Respondents were rated as having increased, remained the same, or decreased in self-esteem on the basis of the amount of change in these scores from first to second administration. Those whose discrepancy score increased 0.5 standard deviations (SD) or more, from first to second administration, were considered to have decreased in self-esteem, those whose discrepancy score decreased 0.5 SD or more were considered to have increased in self-esteem, and those whose discrepancy score neither increased nor decreased by at least 0.5 SD were considered to have remained the same in self-esteem.

The MMPI is a widely used measure of psychological and behavioral adjustment (Dahlstrom & Welsh, 1960). Results on this test are usually interpreted by plotting the scores of ten clinical scales on a standard form, and noting the configuration of the resulting profile. After plotting the profiles of our respondents for the first and second administration of the MMPI, we presented them to eight clinical psychologists (two with Ph.D.s and considerable experience, and six advanced graduate students), and asked them to rate the respondents as improved or not improved from first to second administration. The judges agreed unanimously on 52.5 per cent of the profiles, and at least five of eight judges agreed on 97.5 per cent. In two cases, only four of eight judges agreed, but, since these included the more experienced judges, these profiles were retained.

The IPAT Anxiety Scale is a 40-item scale designed to measure "free floating anxiety," a high degree of which the authors suggest is a common element in all forms of mental disorder, and a low degree of which indicates mental health (Cattell & Scheier, 1963). A respondent was categorized as having decreased in anxiety from first to second administration if her second administration score was 0.5 SD lower than her first administration score, to have increased if it was 0.5 SD higher, and to have remained the same if it was neither 0.5 SD above or below her first administration score.

Finally, two other scales were utilized to determine the degree to which the institution was successful in attaining its goal of people-changing. These were two Guttman scales developed by Rosenberg (1965) to measure faith in people and self-esteem. These scales were administered only once, and thus utilized in cross-sectional analysis. They were chosen for several reasons. Utilizing the theory of differential opportunity systems, Morris (1964) has suggested that the differential rate of delinquency among males and females, and the different types of offenses committed by them are related to different sex role objectives and access to these objectives provided by our society. Her dissertation provides evidence which supports the theory that male delinquency is largely a response to problems related to the achievement of status goals, while female delinquency is largely a response to problems related to the achievement of "relational goals" (the ability to establish close and harmonious relationships with others). Faith in people, we suggest, is one prerequisite for the achievement of such goals. Furthermore, several authors (Hersko, 1964; Konopka, 1966; Kopp, 1960) have noted that delinquent girls are characterized by low self-esteem. Morris' (1964) finding that delinquent girls seem particularly careless about personal grooming when compared to nondelinquent girls or boys, and even to delinquent boys, would seem to support these observations. If we accept Morris' explanation that female delinquency is a response to frustrated attempts to attain relational goals, we can better understand the association of low self-esteem and female delinquency. In his study of over 5,000 high school juniors and seniors, Rosenberg (1965) presents rather convincing evidence that persons with low self-esteem have a good deal of difficulty in interpersonal relations. In light of these studies, we reasoned that if the institution were going to change the girls so that they might function effectively on the outside, its program should serve to increase their faith in people, and their self-esteem. The institution does, in fact, consciously attempt to accomplish this through its program.

After slight modification, both scales yielded a coefficient of reproducibility of 0.92, and a minimal marginal reproducibility of 0.68, utilizing the Cornell Technique. On the basis of profile types, the respondents were classified as having low, medium, or high faith in people, and as being low, medium, or high in self-esteem.

The relationship of change in the girls to five variables other than identification was also investigated, utilizing chi-square analysis. These variables were intelligence quotient, social class, religion, age at entrance, and length of stay in the institution. None of the first three variables were significantly ($p < 0.05$) related to any of the measures of change or of identification. Since we found both length of stay and age at entrance to be significantly related to change and identification, however, we controlled for these two variables in our analyses.[7]

RESULTS

As Table 1 indicates, those girls who identify most highly with the institution are most likely to have high faith in people, and least likely to have low faith in people. The relationship holds both for girls admitted prior to and after age $15^1/_2$ ($N=48$ and 54, respectively) with approximately the same strength (gamma=0.52 and 0.64, respectively).[8] The relationship between institutional identification and faith in people also holds for those ($N=57$) resident 0–12 months, and for those ($N=45$) resident over 12 months, although it is considerably stronger for the latter (gam-

TABLE 1
FAITH IN PEOPLE BY
INSTITUTIONAL IDENTIFICATION

Faith in people	Institutional identification		
	High ($N=34$)	Medium ($N=33$)	Low ($N=35$)
High	35%	21%	11%
Medium	56	52	51
Low	9	27	37
Total %	100	100	99

Gamma=.43.

[7]Originally, we had intended to test the relationship of both identification with staff and with the institution to each of the five measures of change in the inmates. However, because of a procedural error, we administered the measure of staff identification to a majority of the girls three months prior to the other instruments. Since several of the girls might have identified or disidentified with the staff in that time, we felt it unwise to test the relationship between identification with staff and four of the measures of change.

[8]To avoid analyzing tables with very small Ns in the cells, institutional identification was dichotomized into high and low in the control tables. It should be noted, therefore, that the gamma values for these tables are not strictly comparable to those in the main tables.

ma=0.42 and 0.71, respectively). The concern for others exhibited by the staff, the training the girls receive in group sessions, and the general norm of "be thy brother's keeper" which is part of the institutional culture, would seem to result in a generally high faith in people, especially for those girls who identify with the institution, and are long-term residents.

As is seen in Table 2, there is only a slight relationship between institutional identification and self-esteem as measured by Rosenberg's scale for the total sample. The results for short-term residents (gamma=0.18), long term residents (gamma=0.08), and older girls (gamma=−0.06) were of the same magnitude. For younger girls, however, there was a relatively strong, positive relationship (gamma=0.52) between institutional identification and self-esteem. Identification was also more strongly related to favorable change for the younger girls on the

TABLE 2
SELF-ESTEEM BY INSTITUTIONAL
IDENTIFICATION

	Institutional identification		
Self-esteem	*High* (N=34)	*Medium* (N=33)	*Low* (N=35)
High	44%	42%	31%
Medium	44	42	49
Low	12	15	20
Total %	100	99	100

Gamma=.17.

MMPI and the Anxiety scale. In addition, length of stay was more strongly related to change on four of the five measures for the younger girls. The apparently greater impact of the institution on younger girls may be attributable to their greater impressionability and willingness to conform to the institution's somewhat authoritarian atmosphere. Of course, it may be that maturation, aside from any institutional effect, accounts for much of the change observed in the younger girls, but we could not effectively control for this variable.

As indicated in Table 3, self-esteem as measured by the ICL is positively related to identification with a staff member. The relationship was also maintained with approximately the same strength when we controlled for age and length of residence (gamma ranging between 0.48 and 0.59 in the four control tables). In describing staff members on the ICL, the girls were particularly likely to picture them as somewhat managerial and autocratic. Comparison of the girls' real and ideal-self descriptions at entrance to the institution and then at second administration of the ICL revealed a general movement toward the managerial-autocratic octant for their own profiles. Apparently, as the girls see themselves becoming more like staff members, their self-esteem increases.

TABLE 3
SELF-ESTEEM BY IDENTIFICATION
WITH STAFF

Self-esteem	Identify with staff (N=67)	Do not identify (N=33)
Increased	36%	15%
Remained same	46	39
Decreased	18	46
Total %	100	100

Gamma=.51.

Table 4 indicates that improvement in the girls' psychological-behavioral adjustment is positively related to institutional identification. Controlling for length of stay, however, we find that for short term residents ($N=52$), institutional identification is only slightly related to improvement on the MMPI (gamma= 0.14). For long term residents ($N=27$), the relationship is relatively strong (gamma=0.43). The relationship is also stronger for younger girls ($N=32$) than it is for those ($N=47$) older at entrance (gamma values were 0.58 and 0.25, respectively).

Finally, Table 5 shows there is a slight relationship between institutional identification and improvement on the IPAT Anxiety Scale. High identifiers are most likely to improve, but equally as likely as low identifiers to grow worse. As was true for the MMPI, when we control for length of stay, the relationship between identification and improvement is stronger for long term residents ($N=31$, gamma=0.55) than it is for short term residents ($N=51$, gamma=0.04), and stronger for those girls admitted prior to age $15\frac{1}{2}$ ($N=33$, gamma=0.59) than it is for those admitted after this age ($N=49$, gamma=-0.04).

TABLE 4
IMPROVEMENT ON MMPI BY
INSTITUTIONAL IDENTIFICATION

	Institutional identification		
MMPI status	High ($N=19$)	Medium ($N=31$)	Low ($N=29$)
Improved	42%	32%	21%
Not improved	58	68	79
Total %	100	100	100

Gamma=.32.

TABLE 5
CHANGE IN ANXIETY BY
INSTITUTIONAL IDENTIFICATION

	Institutional identification		
Anxiety	High ($N=25$)	Medium ($N=28$)	Low ($N=29$)
Decreased	48%	18%	24%
Remained same	28	50	52
Increased	24	32	24
Total %	100	100	100

Gamma=.16.

In summary, five "tests" of the hypothesis that identification (institutional identification in four instances, and identification with staff in one) is positively related to the amount and type of change experienced by inmates in a correctional setting yielded results in the expected direction for the total population, although the relationship was rather weak in two instances. Even in these instances, however, a strong relationship between identification and change was found for girls who entered the institution at a relatively young age. We would conclude, therefore, that people-changing institutions will attain their goal to the extent that their programs foster identification. We now turn to an analysis of some of the mechanisms by which the institution under study was able to do this.

The Development of Identification

We suggest that identification is facilitated by a relatively structured social environment—i.e., an environment in which behavior is predictable, norms and behavior expectations are clear, and conforming behavior is rather consistently rewarded while non-conforming behavior is consistently punished.

Because of its highly structured program, the institution in question is apparently rather successful in fostering identification with individual staff members and with institutional norms and values. Of the 100 girls for whom we have complete data, 67 identified with the staff member they described on the ICL. This compares favorably with the girls' identification with their parents as indicated by the initial administration of the ICL upon their admission to the institution. At that time, 48.6 per cent of 105 girls for whom we have data identified with their mothers, and 50.5 per cent of 104 girls identified with their fathers.[9]

On the basis of a cross-sectional analysis of Institutional Identification Scale scores (see Table 6), and interviews with the

TABLE 6
INSTITUTIONAL IDENTIFICATION BY
LENGTH OF STAY

Institutional identification	Length of stay in months		
	17 & over (N=39)	7–16 (N=36)	0–6 (N=28)
High	62%	19%	11%
Medium	33	31	36
Low	5	50	54
Total %	100	100	101

Gamma=.64.

[9]Data from the girls' records and interviews indicate that, compared to their institutional experience, the girls' home life was relatively unstructured, being characterized by a plurality of parents and pseudo-parents who issued few or contradictory behavior directives. A gross indicator of the girls' chaotic home life is that 25.2 per cent had lived in five or more family constellations prior to coming to the institution, and 65.5 per cent had lived in at least three.

girls, we would also conclude that institutional identification was fostered by the institution's program. We have suggested that one of the factors conducive to identification is the clarity of institutional social structure and role expectations. Just as important for identification as the degree to which a social system is structured, of course, is the nature of the social interaction which takes place within that system. Many closed institutions present highly structured programs for their inmates, but do not foster identification with staff members or with the institution itself. The girls identify not only because the institution presents a structured environment, but also because staff and peers exhibit genuine concern for their welfare. Mindful of the girls' position, the staff does attempt to treat them as individuals, and is predisposed to be reasonable, loving, and supportive, within the limits set by the rules and nature of the institution. Given these necessary preconditions, a highly structured setting becomes the sufficient condition facilitating identification.

Several mechanisms of social control are employed by the institution which serve to structure social relations in a definite pattern, so that behavioral and attitudinal norms flow primarily from staff to inmates, and from older, staff-oriented inmates to newer inmates. One of these mechanisms is the rule of silence. Girls are expected to maintain silence for all but approximately two hours per day. The rule of silence is enforced most strictly in the dormitory, where the girls are also expected not to "pay attention" to one another. That is, they are expected to avoid even eye contact with one another. Officially maintained as a means of instilling self-discipline, the rule of silence has the obvious effect of facilitating verbal control over a large group of teenage girls, and of focusing their attention on the tasks at hand. More importantly, it also serves to reduce peer interaction, and to channelize it into those time periods and those places where it can best be supervised. The development and maintenance of a deviant peer subculture under these conditions is thus made very difficult.

In general, our data indicate that the peer subculture is primarily staff-oriented. One indication of this is the results obtained by an analysis of peer identification. Besides asking the girls to describe a staff member on the second administration of the ICL, we also asked them to describe, "the girl here at

(institution) who is the most important and meaningful to you."
Of the 67 girls named, only four received four or more nomina-
tions. Three of these four girls were seniors, and one was a junior
who was a resident for over two years. All four had acted in the
capacity of group leader three or more times, all had high
institutional identification scores, and all identified with the staff
member they described on the ICL. Three were high conformers
to institutional norms, and one was a medium conformer. In all,
43 of 115 girls were identified with by one or more of their peers.
As Table 7 indicates, compared to those who are not identified
with, these girls are more likely to be long-term resident upper-
classmen who identify with the staff and the institution, are group
leaders, and relatively high conformers to the institutional norms.

Another important mechanism of social control is the demerit, pink slip, and gold star system. This system of punishment and
reward is the chief means by which a daily record of the girls'
activities as individuals, and as class groups, is recorded. For
minor infractions of institutional norms, demerits are issued by
the staff, while major infractions merit a pink slip. At the end of
each day, the list of demerits and pink slips, the name of the girl
involved, and the nature of the infraction, is read to all the girls
assembled in a large study hall. Individual and class ratings of
"excellent" to "poor" are also given during these sessions, based
upon the girls' performance in their classrooms for the day. The
major effect of either the demerit or the pink slip is that they take
away a girl's gold star for the month, the latter being a symbol of
perfect conduct. Girls who accumulate a given number of gold
stars are eligible for various outings held during the year, and for
other privileges. Gold stars are officially awarded only four or
five times a year, in a ceremony presided over by the Directress
of Girls.

The girls' conduct, then, is constantly being observed and
evaluated. The conference at the end of the day is a structurally
imposed examination of conscience. Whether or not a particular
girl has received a mark that day, she is reminded of the rules and
of what the staff considers acceptable or unacceptable behavior.
Since the honor system is employed, girls do report themselves
during conference for rule infractions which went unnoticed or
unheeded by others.

For many of the girls, participating in a social system in

TABLE 7
CHARACTERISTICS OF GIRLS WHO ARE AND ARE NOT IDENTIFIED WITH BY PEERS

Characteristics	Girls identified with		Girls not identified with	
	%	(Total N)	%	(Total N)
Leaders	48	(42)	24	(58)
Low conformers	16	(43)	35	(57)
High institutional identification	41	(39)	25	(60)
Identify with staff	77	(43)	63	(67)
Resident 0–6 months	14	(43)	32	(72)
Seniors or juniors	46	(43)	36	(72)

which rules of conduct are clearly stated, repeated frequently, and enforced is a relatively new experience. Asked "Considering your life at home, and your life here at (institution), what things would you say are most different?," the modal responses of the fifty girls interviewed fell into two categories. First, they noted, there was more discipline at the institution, that is, one had to do what one was told to do, and second, there was more of a set routine, or "planned and guided rules." The institution's program did appear to have a greater impact on those girls coming from a more unstructured social background. We divided our respondents into two groups on the basis of the number of family constellations they had lived in prior to coming to the institution.[10] Those girls ($N=41$) who lived in two or fewer constellations were considered to have structured backgrounds, and those ($N=78$) who lived in three or more were considered to have unstructured backgrounds. While girls from structured and unstructured backgrounds were about equally likely to identify with staff, and to have high institutional identification scores, identification was more strongly related to change for girls coming from unstructured backgrounds. The results of our analysis are summarized in Table 8. As indicated by the values for gamma, identification is more strongly related to positive change (improvement) on each of the five measures of change for girls from unstructured backgrounds. These results suggest that a relatively structured environment is important both for identification, and for effective socialization, i.e., for people-changing.[11]

[10]A "family" constellation was defined to be any living situation (including institutional) which a girl experienced for a period of at least one month, and in which she was supervised by one or more adults. Thus, if a girl lived with both natural parents for ten years, with only one natural parent for one year, with a parent and step-parent for six months, and in a mental institution for six months, she was classified as having lived in four family constellations.

[11]Some caution would be wise in evaluating these findings. The number of cases considered is small. Moreover, our measure of the relative "structuredness" of a girl's background was rather crude, taking into account primarily the number of family constellations reported in her case record (or self-reported in a few instances where no data were available in the record). No precise measure of the length of time in each constellation, nor the nature of social interaction within each of these constellations could be taken into account. Finally, the greater amount of improvement exhibited by the "unstructured" girls on Rosenberg's Self-Esteem Scale and on the MMPI may in part be an artifact of their initially poorer scores on these instruments. There were, however, no initial differences between the two groups on any of the other scales.

TABLE 8

IMPACT OF IDENTIFICATION* ON GIRLS FROM STRUCTURED AND UNSTRUCTURED BACKGROUNDS

	Structured		Unstructured	
"Change" variable	N	Gamma (ID × Change)	N	Gamma (ID × Change)
Faith in people	35	.25	68	.52
Self-esteem (Rosenberg)	35	−.02	67	.30
Self-esteem (ICL)	33	.32	67	.59
MMPI	24	.19	55	.30
Anxiety	28	−.34	54	.38

*Identification for the ICL is identification with staff member. For all other variables it is institutional identification.

The Directress of Girls estimates that it takes three to six months for a girl to adjust to the institution (during which time she is somewhat rebellious), six months to "find herself," and six months during which she becomes an active, contributing member of the organization. Our observation suggests that, in order not to be won over to staff values and goals, a girl must remain isolated both from staff and from peers. Since this is a closed institution, in which the girls' entire existence is lived, such isolation is difficult to maintain. Again and again in the interviews, the girls cited the inescapable fact that they would be in residence for 18 to 24 months (the normal length of stay before a girl is considered for release) as a reason for a change in behavior and attitudes. To "fight the system" for this period of time would require an heroic effort, especially when one must do it without general peer support.

The absence of alternative reference groups also contributes to the girls' institutional identification. Since this is a closed institution, staff and inmates are the only immediate reference groups available to the girls. As we have indicated, the staff is in rather complete control of the institutional culture, and peer culture offers no effective alternative to staff norms. There are few other groups to which a girl may turn to support anti-staff norms. Parental visits are limited to one per month, and the girls are counseled not to dwell on institutional experiences at these times. Incoming and outgoing mail is censored, so that the girls are also isolated from contrary norms from other outside sources.

Besides the somewhat negative mechanisms of social control outlined above, there are several other mechanisms which more positively involve the girls in the staff's norm and value system. One of these is the monitor system. A system of monitorship is employed in many correctional institutions, including those at the custodial and treatment ends of the continuum. At its worst, it involves corruption and the exploitation of one inmate by another. At its best, it is an effective tool for rehabilitation, since it places the inmate in the staff member's position, and allows him to play a staff role. Staff attitudes and values are thus more readily understood and assimilated as one's own.

Even more than the monitor system, the use of group leaders serves to place inmates in staff roles. Each of the school classes, from Freshman to Senior, meets once a week under the supervision of one of the nuns, known as a group mother. The group mother is assigned to a class for one year, and is assisted in her duties by two girls, titled the group leader and assistant group leader. These girls are elected each month by their peers from a list of those who have indicated their willingness to serve in this capacity. The list is subject to the approval of the Directress of Girls. Once elected, the group leader is responsible for everything her group and its individual members do or fail to do. Her duties involve doing what she can to help her girls "keep their marks down," getting them to the right place at the right time, seeing that any special activities assigned to or planned by the group are carried out, keeping the group's morale high, and getting them to function as a unit. Above all, she is expected to set the example of good attitude and conduct for the girls under her charge. Charged with enforcing the institution's rules, with setting the example of proper behavior for her peers, and with assisting them to live up to staff expectations, a group leader finds it difficult not to accept staff norms and values. A majority of the girls do serve as group leader at least once during their stay.

The group meetings themselves contribute to the girls' identification with the institution. While they are used to disseminate staff directives and information regarding program scheduling, and so forth, the girls also use them to plan various group projects and extracurricular activities. The primary purpose of the meetings, however, is to focus on the group's behavior during the week, as indicated by its record of demerits and pink slips, and to work out ways to improve this record. The meetings also focus on the behavior of individuals. A girl who has been troublesome during the week may be called upon by the group leader to explain her behavior. Group members may then comment upon this behavior, analyzing the reasons behind it, and suggesting ways of improving it. Numerous studies of small groups have indicated that group discussion is important in fostering individual commitment to group goals, and that it is more effective in changing norms than other forms of persuasion, such as lectures or directives (Hare, 1962). By involving each girl in planning for class activities, and in an attempt to keep the group's "marks" down and "build the group up," the meetings contribute to the girls' identification with staff values, and with the institution itself.

Finally, the staff utilizes work assignments (called charges) to permit the girls to increase in status during their stay. The interview material indicates that the girls are aware of a charge hierarchy, and of what one must do to be assigned to a desired charge. The charge system provides a means by which a girl may advance during her stay from responsibility over things to responsibility over people, and from relatively little to relatively great autonomy and trust.

The mechanisms of social control we have outlined above describe a somewhat authoritarian, though benevolent, social system. Newer inmates generally rebelled against these mechanisms, but long-term residents generally were favorable to them, and some even enthusiastic about them. While we have suggested that these mechanisms fostered identification, they are not without dysfunctional potentialities. While the gold star system provided an incentive to many to "prove themselves" and to win staff approval and other rewards by good behavior, it was cited by some as the reason they stopped trying to live up to staff expectations, since gold stars were too easily lost for minor rule infractions which the girls themselves did not define as wrong. Group meetings could and sometimes did deteriorate into sessions in which a girl's ego was "torn down." The situation and responsibilities of monitors and group leaders could lead to discouragement and disillusionment when peers did not cooperate, and in spite of the prestige and privileges which attached to these positions, some girls shunned them. In general, however, these mechanisms did appear to be effective in fostering identification, both with staff members and with the institution.

SUMMARY AND DISCUSSION

We have suggested that the degree to which individuals are changed by correctional institutions is related to the extent to which they identify with staff members, and with the institutional program. Data from a treatment-oriented institution serving delinquent females lend support to this hypothesis.

We have further suggested that correctional institutions may exercise a great deal of control over the extent to which their inmates identify. Given a setting in which administration and staff are benevolent and mindful of inmate status, such factors as clear organizational structure and role expectations, long length of anticipated and actual stay, few alternative reference groups, high organizational participation, and readily available channels for organizational mobility are conducive to identification. A brief description of several mechanisms of social control employed by the study institution served to illustrate these points.

It should be noted, however, that the same highly structured program would not necessarily be equally successful with other populations, and that other types of programs might be equally successful. The Highfields program (McCorkle et al., 1958), and particularly the Provo Experiment (Empey & Rabow, 1961), achieve similar results by thrusting the delinquent into a relatively *unstructured* social system, placing the responsibility for rehabilitation, from the beginning, on the individual himself. These programs serve delinquent males. Perhaps it is precisely because of the difference in male and female psychology and socialization that these different programs appear to result in equal success. The study institution's program of total environmental control would perhaps meet with much stronger opposition from a delinquent male population. Likewise, we suspect its attempts to isolate dissident inmates from one another and to prevent the development of a deviant peer subculture would be less successful in an institution serving males. Studies of institutions serving females reveal an inmate subculture composed primarily of couples, and an underlying lack of trust, or at least an expectation of "betrayal" on the part of fellow inmates. This type of inmate social structure is more amenable to staff control than the more pervasive inmate social structure which appears to be characteristic of institutions serving males, and is thus more responsive to a highly structured program.

Finally, we must note that the factors considered conducive to identification were isolated on the basis of a review of varied literature and the empirical study of but one organization. Further research will be necessary to determine to what extent and under what conditions these factors are operative in other organizations.

References

Adamek, R. J. 1965. The positional identification of adults. Mimeographed.

Berk, B. B. 1966. Organizational goals and inmate organization. *American Journal of Sociology* 71:522–34.

Blum, A. 1962. Peer group and a child's verbal accessibility in a treatment institution. *Social Service Review* 36:385–95.

Cattell, R. B., and I. H. Scheier. 1963. *Handbook for the IPAT anxiety scale questionnaire*. Champaign, Ill.: Institute for Personality and Ability Testing.

Clemmer, D. 1958. *The prison community*. New York: Rinehart.

Cressey, D. R. 1955. Changing criminals: The application of the theory of differential association. *American Journal of Sociology* 61:116–20.

Dahlstrom, W. G., and G. S. Welsh. 1960. *An MMPI handbook*. Minneapolis: University of Minnesota Press.

Edwards, A. L. 1957. *Techniques of attitude scale construction*. New York: Appleton-Century-Crofts.

Empey, L. T., and J. Rabow. 1961. The Provo experiment in delinquency rehabilitation. *American Sociological Review* 26:679–96.

Engh, J. 1966. New hope for girls in trouble. *U.S. Catholic* 31:37–42.

Eshleman, J. R.; A. E. Havens; and H. R. Potter. 1960. Construction of an identification scale. Unpublished paper. Columbus: The Ohio State University.

Etzioni, A. 1961. *A comparative analysis of complex organizations*. New York: The Free Press.

Fiedler, F. E. 1953. The psychological-distance dimension in interpersonal relations. *Journal of Personality* 22:142–50.

Fisher, S. 1961. Social organization in a correctional residence. *The Pacific Sociological Review* 4:87–93.

Garabedian, P. G. 1963. Social roles and processes of socialization in the prison community. *Social Problems* 11:139–52.

Giallombardo, Rose. 1966. *Society of women: A study of a women's prison*. New York: Wiley.

Goffman, E. 1961. *Asylums*. Garden City, N. Y.: Anchor Books, Doubleday.

Grosser, G. H. 1958. The role of informal inmate groups in change of values. *Children* 5:25–29.

Grusky, O. 1959. Organizational goals and the behavior of informal leaders. *American Journal of Sociology* 65:59–67.

Grusky, O. 1962. Authoritarianism and effective indoctrination: A case study. *Administrative Science Quarterly* 7:79–95.

Hare, A. P. 1962. *Handbook of small group research*. New York: The Free Press of Glencoe.

Heffernan, Sister M. Esther. 1964. Inmate social systems and sub-systems: The square, the cool, and the life. Ph.D. dissertation. Washington, D. C.: Catholic University of America.

Hersko, M. 1964. Community therapy in an institution for delinquent girls. *Federal Probation* 28:41–46.

Jourard, S. M. 1957. Identification, parent cathexis, and self-esteem. *Journal of Consulting Psychology* 21:375–80.

Konopka, Gisela. 1966. *The adolescent girl in conflict*. Englewood Cliffs, N. J.: Prentice-Hall.

Kopp, Sister Mary Audrey. 1960. Anomic pressure and deviant behavior. *The Sociological Quarterly* 1:226–38.

Kosofsky, S., and A. Ellis. 1958. Illegal communication among institutionalized female delinquents. *The Journal of Social Psychology* 48:155–60.

Leary, T. 1957. *Interpersonal diagnosis of personality.* New York: Ronald Press.

Leary, T. 1956. *Multilevel measurement of interpersonal behavior.* Berkeley: Psychological Consultation Service.

McCorkle, L. W.; A. Elias; and F. L. Bixby. 1958. *The highfields story.* New York: Holt.

McCorkle, L. W., and R. Korn. 1954. Resocialization within the walls. *The Annals of the American Academy of Political and Social Sciences* 293:88–89.

Miller, D. 1964. *Growth to freedom.* London: Tavistock.

Morris, Ruth R. 1964. Female delinquency and relational problems. *Social Forces* 43:82–89.

Ohlin, L. E., and W. C. Lawrence. 1959. Social interaction among clients as a treatment problem. *Social Work* 4:3–13.

Polsky, H. 1962. *Cottage six.* New York: Russell Sage Foundation.

Rosenberg, M. 1965. *Society and the adolescent self-image.* Princeton, N. J.: Princeton University Press.

Street, D. P. 1965. Inmates in custodial and treatment settings. *American Sociological Review* 30:40–55.

Street, D. P.; R. D. Vinter; and C. Perrow. 1967. *Organization for treatment.* New York: The Free Press.

Sykes, G. M. 1958. *The society of captives.* Princeton, N. J.: Princeton University Press.

Thompson, Dorothy J. 1961. The psychology of the Good Shepherd nuns in the re-education of the emotionally disturbed. M.A. thesis. San Antonio: St. Mary's University.

Vinter, R. D. 1963. Analysis of treatment organizations. *Social Work* 8:3–15.

Vinter, R. D., and M. Janowitz. 1959. Effective institutions for juvenile delinquents: A research statement. *Social Service Review* 33:118–30.

Ward, D. A., and G. C. Kassebaum. 1965. *Women's prison: Sex and the social structure.* Chicago: Aldine.

Wheeler, S. 1961. Socialization in correctional communities. *American Sociological Review* 26:706–11.

Winch, R. F. 1962. *Identification and its familial determinants.* Indianapolis: Bobbs-Merrill.